IT Business Management

Solutions from SAP - A Pocket Guide

Other publications by Van Haren Publishing

Van Haren Publishing (VHP) specializes in titles on Best Practices, methods and standards within four domains:
- IT management
- Architecture (Enterprise and IT)
- Business management and
- Project management

VHP is also publisher on behalf of leading companies and institutions:
The Open Group, IPMA-NL, PMI-NL, CA, Getronics, Quint, ITSqc, LLC, The Sox Institute and ASL BiSL Foundation

Topics are (per domain):

IT (Service) Management / IT Governance	Architecture (Enterprise and IT)	Project/Programme/ Risk Management
ASL	Archimate®	A4-Projectmanagement
BiSL	GEA®	ICB / NCB
CATS	TOGAF™	MINCE®
CMMI		M_o_R®
CobiT		MSP™
ISO 17799	**Business Management**	*PMBOK® Guide*
ISO 27001	EFQM	PRINCE2™
ISO 27002	eSCM	
ISO/IEC 20000	ISA-95	
ISPL	ISO 9000	
IT Service CMM	ISO 9001:2000	
ITIL® V3	OPBOK	
ITSM	SixSigma	
MOF	SOX	
MSF	SqEME®	
ABC of ICT	eSCM	
SABSA		

For the latest information on VHP publications, visit our website: www.vanharen.net.

IT Business Management

Management

Solutions from SAP - A Pocket Guide

Swen Conrad, PMP
David Pultorak

COLOFON

Title:	IT Business Management
	Solutions from SAP - A Pocket Guide
Series:	Best Practice
Authors:	Swen Conrad, PMP, Senior Marketing Director, IT Business Management, SAP AG
	David Pultorak, CEO, Pultorak & Associates, Ltd.
Text edit:	Barbara Kendrick, TDA Group
Publisher:	Van Haren Publishing, Zaltbommel-NL, www.vanharen.net
ISBN:	978 90 8753 620 6
Print:	First edition, first impression, October 2010
Layout and design:	CO2 Premedia bv, Amersfoort -- NL
Copyright:	© 2010 Van Haren Publishing

For further enquiries about Van Haren Publishing, please send an e-mail to: info@vanharen.net
This publication has been composed with utmost care; however, neither Author nor Editor nor Publisher can accept any liability for damage caused by possible errors and/or incompleteness in this publication.
No part of this publication may be reproduced in any form by print, photo print, microfilm or any other means without written permission by the Publisher.

CONTENTS

FOREWORD

When SAP started 35 years ago, IT was a back-office function aimed more at efficiency than transformation. Compared to today, systems were straightforward and self-contained, and IT management was focused inwardly on programming and maintenance.

Over the years, our industry has increased the scope of its focus, maturity, and capability to manage complex applications, infrastructure, and IT services. We work hard to meet expanding expectations and escalating constraints with innovative technologies and rigorous approaches to managing enterprise architecture, customer demand, project and service portfolios, solution development, and operations.

Ultimately, we try to run our IT organization like a real business – to drive business results and create business value with IT functionality. But we are often challenged because our IT management solutions don't provide the kind of insight needed to drive decisions that cut cost, streamline operations, control risk and improve our understanding of IT performance.

Managing IT like a business demands integrated and systematic business and IT insight – the kind of integration and systematic insight that SAP has spent the last 35 years helping the world's leading companies achieve. Best-run businesses use SAP® solutions to automate key business processes so they can close the gap between strategy and execution. Best-run businesses drive clarity into their organizations by gaining insight for improved performance, efficiency for optimized operations, and flexibility to adapt quickly to changing circumstances.

Like best-run businesses, best-run IT organizations are able to optimize operations, maximize innovation, and adjust rapidly to evolving business needs. Their IT management solutions help them better understand themselves and their customers and make the best decisions in the face of challenging expectations and constraints.

SAP can help you become a best-run IT organization. We offer robust software tools, best-practice guidance, expert services, and predefined key performance indicators spanning IT performance and governance, portfolio and project management, resource management, IT service management, application lifecycle management, and more. Our toolset is flexible and powerful, so you can progress incrementally and achieve a unique level of integration between business processes and IT capability.

This book outlines SAP's view on best-run IT. It will help orient you to our related solutions and provide you with ideas for driving clarity and business value in your IT organization. On behalf of myself and all my colleagues across the SAP organization who contributed to this book and are driving the topic of IT business management at SAP forward, I welcome all our fellow IT professionals to join us on our journey toward integrated IT management. Our mutual goal is to drive enterprise performance and business value for our valued customers.

Jérôme Levadoux
SVP & General Manager
IT Business Management
SAP AG

KEY CONTRIBUTORS

Jonathan Becher
EVP Marketing, SAP AG

Oliver Bussmann
EVP & CIO, SAP AG

Richard Campione
EVP & General Manager, Line of Business Solutions, SAP AG

Chris Horak
VP Marketing, SAP NetWeaver, SAP AG

Kevin Ichhpurani,
SVP Business Development & Strategic Alliances, SAP AG

Bryan Katis
VP Solution Management, Enterprise Performance Management, SAP AG

Jérôme Levadoux
SVP & General Manager, IT Business Management, SAP AG

Lori Mitchell-Keller
SVP Solution Management, Idea-to-Delivery, SAP AG

Prakash Nanduri
VP Corporate Strategy, SAP AG

Dr. Klaus Schmelzeisen
VP Professional Services, IT Transformation, SAP AG

Ulrich Scholl
VP Marketing, IT Business Management, SAP AG

Jujhar Singh
SVP Solution Management, Self-Service & Marketing, SAP AG

1. BUSINESS VALUE AND THE IT ORGANIZATION

1.1 Where We are Today

In the 1980s, businesses everywhere moved to information technology (IT) as a way to do more work with greater speed at lower risk. In those days, companies made IT investments with considerable caution, focusing largely on the issues of efficiency and control.

IT became a force in business in the 1990s when companies used it to transform how they worked and interacted with customers. Investments in IT were liberal, buoyed by a healthy economy and concerns about lagging behind the competition. IT management focused on nimble implementations of new software to support new capabilities.

Today, IT reflects aspects of both eras, with companies aiming to improve efficiency and reduce cost while enabling transformative innovation at the same time. Unfortunately, technology alone is not the difference-maker it once was. As IT has become increasingly commoditized on various fronts, companies have fewer opportunities to lap competitors purely on the basis of the solutions they decide to implement.

At the same time, organizations face greater regulatory hurdles than ever before, many of which intersect with how they manage their IT environments. Complying with these regulations requires companies to execute business processes and track information in ways that often impede flexibility and escalate operating costs while also adding risks of noncompliance.

Add to this a renewed focus on cost controls that constrain resources and curb the appetite for bold investment, and it's easy to see why many IT organizations feel under siege as they struggle to justify their value to the business.

In an era of commoditized technology, growing compliance obligations, and limited resources, what can IT organizations do to succeed? What does success even look like?

1.2   Efficiency and Innovation

If yours is like most IT organizations, operational efficiency is high on your list of goals. You want to work smart, make good decisions, and maximize your resources. You also want your costs – and your risks – to be as clear and controllable as possible.

But is efficiency by itself good enough for IT in today's business world? The simple answer is no. Today, companies seek to wield IT as a competitive weapon – one that enables innovation and helps the business do what it does better than anyone else. To rise to the occasion, your IT organization needs to get closer to the business so that it can understand what drives enterprise performance. All of the decisions you make – both large and small – must be made in the context of a simple question: how can IT support strategic innovation for the business it serves?

These two aspects of IT success – efficiency and innovation – feed off one another in a virtuous cycle. Greater efficiency frees up budget, resources, and capacity to dedicate to innovation – innovation that makes IT more effective *and* helps the business execute on strategy. As it becomes more efficient, IT earns the trust of the business. This helps to bring IT closer to the business so that it can better understand where to aim its innovation. The net result is that IT adds value to the business. Instead of a cost center that needs to be cut, IT is viewed as a contributor to enterprise performance that is worthy of ongoing investment.

1.3   Maximizing the Value of Scarce Resources

The question remains: How do you do it? How do you successfully optimize operations and drive innovation to support business strategy? For more and more CIOs, the answer is to run IT as a business to direct and optimize the use of scarce IT resources. But what exactly does this mean?

Consider the scenario of an online retailer who does more than 75 percent of its yearly business during the month of December as customers shop for Christmas. To prepare for the increased demand, the business ensures that enough product is on hand, while IT ensures that it has the server capacity to handle the increased traffic. In the past, let's say that IT maintained 100 servers for the entire year, with 75 percent of them sitting dormant for 11 months. This, IT reasoned, was the cost of doing business. And without the business side closely monitoring IT costs, this approach worked fine.

Today, of course, most businesses are extremely cost-conscious. Fortunately, multiple solutions now exist that can help IT address the issue of server demand more cost-effectively. For example, the company could invest in virtualization technology to expand capacity without additional hardware. It could also reserve cloud resources for the expected period of increased demand. But before making a decision, the business will want to fully understand the trade-offs involved. What is the cost of maintaining under-utilized server capacity for 11 months of the year compared to the cost of the alternatives? How long will it take to recoup any investment made in virtualization? What are the risks of running internal business processes in the context of server capacity that is outsourced to the cloud? If the company deviates from traditional practices, does it stand to lose valuable customers? If so, will the cost savings outweigh the potential loss?

An IT organization that runs itself as a business is able to answer these questions and advise the larger organization on the best course of action. As with any other business, IT's advice is based on the expected business benefit and the related resource requirements regarding cost and capacity constraints, as well as the ability to deliver and the overall risk.

Once a decision is made, IT then needs the ability to take prompt and effective action, monitor performance, and make improvements where necessary. In the end, IT acts as any business doing its best to create value and deliver it to its customer.

Value, of course, cannot be approached as a one-off endeavor. To stay in business, IT needs to deliver value on an ongoing basis. This makes value creation the lens through which IT must view the entire portfolio of its activities and investments as it attempts to run itself as a business.

Especially when looking at the complete portfolio of IT activities and assets, and putting them in order of decreasing value, it will be very obvious where to direct scarce IT resources: to the projects, activities, or applications that add the highest value. And while this may sound harsh, it may be better to cut lower-value activities, applications, or services rather than let them dilute the overall value of your IT department.

There is only one broad exception to the simple math of the IT cost-to-value calculation: IT risk.

1.4   IT Risk Drives Business Risk

Managing IT as a business aims to increase the ratio of IT business value to IT cost. The goal is to grow this key ratio over time and to understand the influencing factors. In other words: Which activities or projects add value? What are the biggest IT cost drivers?

But despite the goal to grow this key performance indicator (KPI) for IT business management, we must also consider associated risks. While minimizing the cost of activities that add lower value (for example, by outsourcing to low-cost providers) may increase this KPI, it may also add significantly to the overall company risk profile. An unfortunate proof is the increasing number of news stories about lost or stolen customer data resulting from outsourcing. The cost of related negative publicity can quickly outweigh the cost savings that outsourcing may deliver.

Now, instead of simply maintaining the status quo or maximizing IT value at all costs, IT must find its own balance between the two extremes. And risk is part of any kind of business equation when a part of the business is trying to go where it has never gone before.

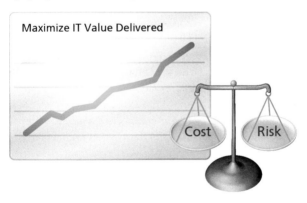

Figure 1.1 The perfect balance of IT value, cost, and risk

So instead of avoiding risk and sticking with the status quo, the new IT paradigm is about *calculating* and *controlling* risk. When you understand the potential negative impact and likelihood of the occurrence of risks, and have a well-defined mitigation plan and ongoing controls in place, these risks are calculated and controlled. With such transparency, you can have an educated discussion and evaluation of the risks and come to a business decision among all the business stakeholders. You are running IT like a business. Figure 1.1 (see previous page) shows the relationship of the three IT business management KPIs: IT value, cost, and risk.

1.5   Managing the Business of IT

To run IT as a business, you need insight first and foremost – insight into business needs and IT capabilities so that you can understand the priorities of your customer (the business) as well as the trade-offs involved in addressing them. You must also have control and the means to act on your insight, so that you can deliver responsive service, mitigate risk, maintain quality, and ensure security.

Like running any business, you also must be smart about how you gather information, execute daily activities, and deliver your services. This requires metrics and analytics to provide insight, comprehensive processes to enable control, and effective automation so that IT can manage enterprise-scale workloads and deliver on a consistent basis.

We have already discussed the requirements for managing IT as a business. They are also well described in ITIL®, Version 3 (ITIL V3). The strong emphasis on business services in ITIL V3 shifts the focus from internal IT services and components to external business services, business results, and outcomes. ITIL V3, in addition to other frameworks like COBIT (Control Objectives for Information and Related Technology), provides a tremendous knowledge base and valuable insight for the ongoing IT business transformation.

Figure 1.2 Services Lifecycle in ITIL V3

As shown in Figure 1.2, the lifecycle in ITIL V3 holistically covers the following five phases:

- **Service strategy** – where the goal is to make IT an integral part of business in order to stop the ongoing competition between business and IT. This will be achieved by a new IT mindset focusing on maximized IT business value – measured in business terms – combined with controlled IT cost and risk. All IT decisions, projects, and activities will be prioritized and managed following this new paradigm, maximizing the utilization of limited resources.
- **Service design and service transition** – where the goal is to properly design, build, and/or source new IT-driven business capabilities based on the strategy direction set above. Resources are only invested in projects and activities that comply with overall company strategy. Execution of these priorities is done in a transparent and effective

fashion. Well-planned and orchestrated deployments bridge the gap between the IT development and operations team, minimizing disruptions to the business and empowering the operations team to successfully run new business solutions.

- **Service operation** – where the goal is to automate – or more accurately industrialize – daily IT activities to minimize cost and effort by the means of auto-detection and resolution of IT alerts, including well-defined workflows. Such proactive management not only saves precious company resources (remember, we are no longer differentiating between business and IT) that can be reallocated to more strategic-level activities. In addition, well-defined and well-executed IT operations and support processes heavily shape the perception of IT through streamlined user interactions.

- **Continual service improvement** – where the goal is to proactively resolve issues, both of potential or systematic nature, by seamlessly feeding operations insight back to the strategy, design, and transition phases. This last, and perhaps most important, phase relies strongly on integrated, end-to-end IT processes that barely exist in corporations today.

The outside-in, results-driven approach starting with business services in mind is the right direction for IT. More and more IT practitioners are adopting this approach, which we like to refer to as the IT nirvana. Due to the highly intangible nature of IT and the complexity of all it comprises, reaching nirvana is a challenge not only for individual practitioners but for the whole industry. And anyone claiming to have got there may have peeled the outer layer of the services lifecycle, but most likely has not connected all the underlying management layers of IT process, application, and infrastructure. This is a complex task and requires broad industry collaboration between the major vendors for hardware, business applications, IT management tools, and IT business management tools.

To make the IT business management challenge more tangible and to be more in sync with commonly used IT management models, we are not going to follow the above model in this book. While the authors believe in its validity, the ITIL V3 model, just like the majority of IT, is too intangible. Therefore, the IT management framework for this book differentiates in the more commonly known categories below:

- **IT business management** – where the goal is to systematically apply commercial principles to IT supply and demand. This means that IT must make choices not focusing on technical merit alone but rather on economic principles. On the flip side, requesters and users of IT must understand and appreciate that the more sophisticated their IT demands are, the more expensive they will be. This advanced insight into IT cost and value will – over time – drive a more thoughtful consumption of IT capabilities.

- **IT service management** – where the goal is to fight the growing IT operations spend by streamlining related processes starting with the IT service desk – the "IT storefront" to the end user. Critical elements are strong process orientation with rule-based workflows; deeper and deeper integration into the more technical layers of IT; self-healing technologies; and increasing process integration beyond the traditional scope of IT service management.

- **Application lifecycle management** – where the goal is to manage the software development lifecycle as well as the end-to-end operation of business applications. Managing these two diverse activities within a single framework and tool will help to bridge the often deep mistrust between application development and operations.

- **Infrastructure management** – where the goal is to optimize IT landscapes for reliability, flexibility, and cost. Increasing encapsulation of technologies into utility or cloud-based service offerings will help to shift the IT focus away from technology to a more business-oriented way of talking and accessing compute resources: "How much storage can I get at what price?" While the make of the storage will matter less and less in future, additional business-relevant criteria such as risk will play an increasing part in the day-to-day infrastructure conversation.

Managing the Business of IT

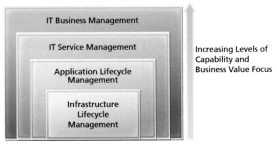

Increasing Levels of Capability and Business Value Focus

Managing IT Components

Figure 1.3 IT evolution – adding a business lens to IT

As shown in Figure 1.3, these IT management disciplines have evolved over time, with the lower levels serving as a foundation for the next higher level of optimization. Here is an example of this evolution.

Many of us will remember about 15 years ago when IT was struggling with frequently failing local area networks. Along with other innovations, this led to the advent of infrastructure management tools. Once this and similar problems on the IT component level were solved, users grew dissatisfied with slow application performance – and application performance management, an important element of application lifecycle management, was born. Next, as IT problems dropped in number and became more random, we stopped seeing IT staff swarming around the building and started wondering how to get support for IT issues, or simply who to call. This drove the need for consistent IT processes enabled by IT service management. And with the IT service management evolving at high speed, many of us are now wondering why – despite all these great optimizations in the past – IT is still so expensive. One of the reasons that IT is expensive is because it has rarely been managed for business benefit or for cost control and containment. Rather, it has usually been managed for maximum performance of IT services, with poor insight into, and therefore poor control of, cost.

Consider this question: Should every application's performance provide the same level of end-user experience? When IT budgets were unlimited, the answer was: Why not? However, with today's cost-consciousness, the answer changes to: Maybe not. Today, the only applications that absolutely must perform speedily and flawlessly are those where flagging performance may interfere with revenue – such as your customer-facing website where you take orders. In that case, the business benefit outweighs the cost of high application performance. For any other applications, it's necessary to compare cost and benefit first!

This basic connection between IT service (including performance characteristics in the previous example) and its relevance to the business has frequently gone unevaluated. Consequently, a lot of work and budget has gone – and is still going – into IT activities and projects with little overall business value.

This is exactly where the evolution of IT toward a business model will make the difference: it will prioritize scarce business resources in a way that maximizes IT output measured in business benefit.

Overall, this challenge is very similar to what other parts of the business experienced years earlier and solved via consolidated enterprise resource planning (ERP) applications. Only time will tell whether the next innovation will lead the industry toward an "ERP for IT."

1.6   Managing IT Supply and Demand

While one of the primary aims of IT today is to run itself as a business, it is equally true that IT still needs to manage the core technology infrastructure, applications, and IT services that have traditionally been its responsibility. What's changed is that IT must do this in a way that focuses on business needs, while communicating to the business in a language that the business can understand. The focus, as stressed before, has shifted from provisioning technology to delivering business services – the business-facing end services that IT customers typically see, recognize, and pay for.

The result is an emerging level of IT management known as IT business management. IT business management should not be confused with the management of business processes, responsibility for which wholly resides within the business itself. Neither should it be confused with managing component subservices such as networking, backup, or testing. This is a part of IT service management, which is the next layer down in the IT management stack (as shown in Figure 1.4). Rather, IT business management focuses on supporting business processes and creating value through the provision of business services such as messaging, collaboration services, and order entry, to name just a few examples. Ultimately, the aim of IT business management is to orient IT externally, according to the business services it delivers to its customer rather than the technology components it manages.

Like any other business, IT must understand both what the customer wants and what it can deliver. For complex businesses and equally complex IT environments, this is no easy task. Hence the emergence of IT demand management as one of the pivotal focus areas for ensuring IT success.

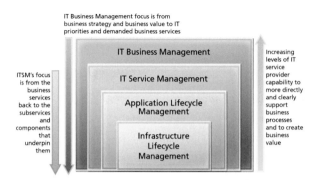

Figure 1.4 Emerging areas of IT Business Management

A number of technologies exist today that expand the scope of IT demand management beyond strategy and tactics to the level of operational execution. These include virtualization, software as a service (SaaS), service-oriented architecture (SOA), cloud computing, service catalogs, service-level management workflows, service monitoring, and control tooling. With these technologies, IT is increasingly able to meet business needs in real time or near real time.

As concluded previously, matching IT demand with limited IT resource supply in a way that maximizes business value forms the next step in IT management's continuing evolution. IT business management emphasizes the delivery of value by understanding the business – its processes, strategies and objectives – and managing IT to support these. IT demand management emphasizes the ability to act on this knowledge by flexibly matching IT resources to business needs from strategy down to real-time operational execution.

Figure 1.5 highlights four key additional architectural elements that help the transformation of IT into IT business management. SAP refers to this group of elements as IT strategy and performance management. The elements are:

- IT strategy, governance, and risk management
- IT portfolio and project management
- IT financial management
- IT workforce and vendor management

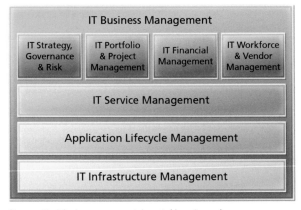

Figure 1.5 Key IT business management elements (shown in green)

As the figure shows and the previous discussion explains, these capabilities do not stand alone. They are an extension of the mostly existing IT management stack, including IT service management, application lifecycle management, and infrastructure management. They add a "business lens" to all the more technical IT activities and processes.

No vendor today can claim to offer an overarching solution that supports end-to-end management of IT supply and demand – what we referred to as "ERP for IT." SAP, however, offers a range of solutions that can help IT run more effectively as a business today and that help you achieve a best-run IT organization.

Today's SAP solutions set the stage for full IT business management capabilities in the near future. This book explores both the current solutions and the SAP vision for managing IT supply and demand, presenting the building blocks that can move you toward achieving a vision for your own IT organization starting today.

2. HOW SAP HELPS: SOLUTIONS FOR IT BUSINESS MANAGEMENT

For more than three decades SAP has helped companies run more effectively with a disciplined focus on consistent yet flexible business processes. These business processes enable companies to operate with greater speed and agility at lower cost, which has become a business necessity for organizations driven by the economic principles of the open market.

Today, these same economic principles are dictating the behavior of IT and how businesses look at the role of IT within the larger organization. As discussed earlier, IT decisions are now driven as much by issues of cost and value as they are by the merits of one technology over another. IT has matured into an entity that can deliver true business value to the organization it serves.

This is why SAP takes seriously the issue of running IT like a business. The problems IT faces today are essentially the same as those faced by the companies SAP has been working with since its inception. With unparalleled business process expertise, SAP – more than any other vendor on the market today – is in a unique position to help.

In this regard, the mission of SAP is to put a business lens on top of existing IT management disciplines to help drive out complexity and enable IT to operate in a way that meets the needs of the company. IT should be able to consume data from lower levels of IT management in a way that enables decision makers to prioritize their activities based on business priorities.

As discussed in more detail in the next section, this can be accomplished with functionality available in the SAP Business Suite applications. In the past, many SAP customers have in fact adapted SAP Business Suite functionality to help them more effectively manage IT. More recently, SAP has taken the initiative to develop specific solution offerings for managing the business of IT.

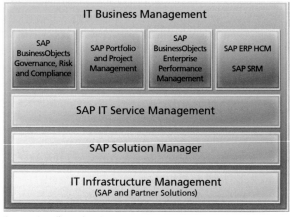

Figure 2.1 SAP offerings for IT business management

Some specific offerings come directly from SAP Business Suite, such as the SAP IT Service Management application and the SAP Solution Manager application management solution. Other solutions are complementary, including some offered by partners in the SAP ecosystem. In addition, a wide range of service offerings is available to help you maximize your investment and ensure success with your initiatives to run IT as a business.

Figure 2.1 provides a quick overview of how these offerings fit together based on the general schema for IT management presented in the previous section. The remainder of this book will dive into some of the specific challenges IT organizations face today. We will explore the ways in which these offerings can help you meet these challenges by driving down IT costs, increasing IT efficiency, and constantly enhancing IT value.

2.1 SAP Business Suite

If you're like many SAP customers, you run your core business processes with SAP Business Suite software – including the SAP ERP, SAP Customer Relationship Management (CRM), SAP Supply Chain Management, SAP Supplier Relationship Management, and SAP Product Lifecycle Management applications. Across a wide range of corporate functions, SAP Business Suite software helps you manage your critical business processes and gain the insight you need to improve performance, optimize operations, and adapt quickly to changing circumstances.

Given the strategic role that SAP Business Suite plays for your company, it is only natural that IT should look for ways to optimize the investment. One way to do this is to leverage SAP Business Suite to manage IT more effectively. After all, maintaining a view of IT that is separate from the business is part of the problem IT faces in the first place. SAP Business Suite, by contrast, supports the kind of integrated approach that businesses demand today.

For example, consider the SAP IT Service Management (SAP ITSM) application, which is part of SAP CRM and integrated with SAP ERP and SAP Solution Manager. This application supports the business processes that enable you to run every aspect of your service desk operations – from managing incidents and problems based on service level agreements, to properly implementing infrastructure changes to eliminate any negative user impact. In much the same way that SAP CRM helps companies interact with their customers and address their needs, so SAP ITSM helps IT interact more effectively with the business to address business needs. What's more, SAP ITSM does this in a way that complies with the best practices articulated in the ITIL V3 framework.

IT service management solutions are widely available from an abundance of vendors, but most of these solutions require investment in software, hardware, and employee skills on top of your existing SAP assets and expertise. Using SAP ITSM lets you standardize in a way that leverages your existing investment in SAP Business Suite software, as well as SAP's long-standing expertise in making business processes work as effectively as possible.

SAP Business Suite also supports another growing need among SAP customers who seek to run IT as a business: a way to integrate traditional IT service management processes with the financial and logistics processes in SAP ERP. This explains why more and more SAP customers are now extending the reach of their SAP Business Suite investment into core IT functions.

Another SAP solution, the SAP Enterprise Asset Management solution, gives IT virtually seamless access to the procurement and receipt of IT equipment. This provides visibility into the true valuation of all the IT assets under management and insight into the status of asset acquisitions in progress. The native integration between SAP solutions provides automatic creation of serial numbers for equipment, allows capitalization as fixed assets if required, and enables synchronization of IT configuration items. This helps IT understand the true cost of services provided and forms the basis for a fair and accurate charge to the various lines of business.

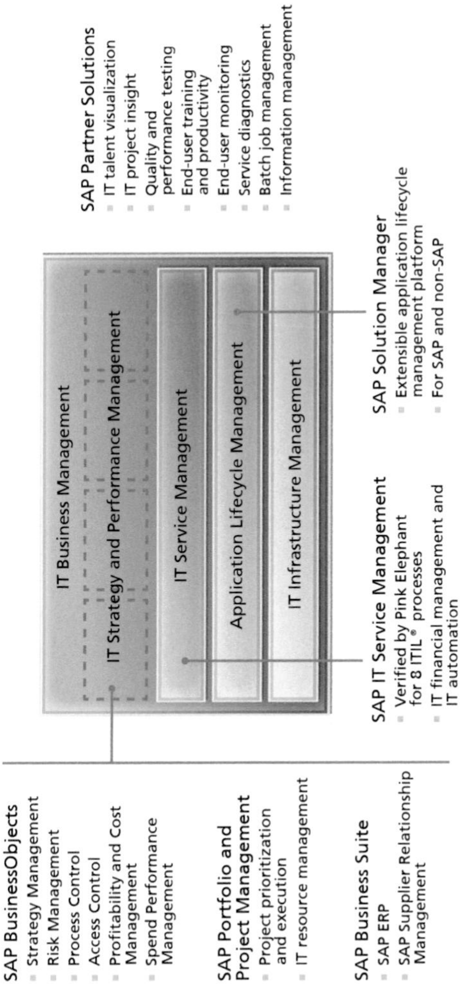

SAP BusinessObjects
- Strategy Management
- Risk Management
- Process Control
- Access Control
- Profitability and Cost Management
- Spend Performance Management

SAP Portfolio and Project Management
- Project prioritization and execution
- IT resource management

SAP Business Suite
- SAP ERP
- SAP Supplier Relationship Management

IT Business Management

IT Strategy and Performance Management

IT Service Management

Application Lifecycle Management

IT Infrastructure Management

SAP IT Service Management
- Verified by Pink Elephant for 8 ITIL® processes
- IT financial management and IT automation

SAP Solution Manager
- Extensible application lifecycle management platform
- For SAP and non-SAP

SAP Partner Solutions
- IT talent visualization
- IT project insight
- Quality and performance testing
- End-user training and productivity
- End-user monitoring
- Service diagnostics
- Batch job management
- Information management

Figure 2.2 IT Management offerings from SAP

The majority of the solutions mentioned above are discussed in more detail throughout this pocket guide. In addition to these, SAP delivers a wide range of other solutions that enables IT to manage its activities more effectively and deliver greater value to the business. Together, these IT solutions from SAP help IT manage activities more intelligently while reducing IT costs, controlling risk, and delivering greater value to the business.

2.2   IT Strategy and Performance

The best IT organizations know exactly what they can
deliver and what they cannot. In areas where an IT
organization excels, it should go to lengths to demonstrate the value this
adds to the business. Where it does not excel, IT should take pains to
develop the required capabilities or find a suitable outsourcing partner to
fill the gap.

The problem for most IT organizations is that they really don't know their
own strengths. Sometimes IT believes that it can deliver on a particular
objective only to be proven wrong. Other times, IT can in fact deliver, but
the costs are too high. Still other times, IT delivers regularly at satisfactory
cost but lacks the metrics to demonstrate this success to the business.
Common to all of these scenarios is a lack of insight stemming from an
inability to adequately account for the activities that make up the bulk of
IT work. As the saying goes, if you can't measure it, you can't manage it.

Take the example of a company with an aggressive growth strategy. Let's
say that this company plans to add 2,000 new employees over the course of
two years, either through direct hire or acquisition. For each new employee
absorbed into the organization, the company must perform a wide range
of tasks. Many of these are conducted by IT, such as provisioning a new
laptop computer, issuing an email address, ordering a new system security
card, and assigning a new cell phone. What exactly are the activities and
sub-activities that go into this employee onboarding process? How much
do they cost? And how does IT measure up to the industry average? Is it
better or worse than the competition?

Answers to these questions can make a tremendous difference to both the
business and IT. Let's say that IT finds that it spends $6,000 to bring a
new employee on board – including process costs as well as the cost of the
new equipment (laptop, cell phone, and so forth). If the company wants

to expand by 2,000 employees, IT should advise the business to add $12 million to the budget just for the onboarding, not counting the day-to-day support and operation of these additional users and systems.

If only it were so easy. The fact is, tracking IT costs is notoriously difficult – which has to do with the nature of IT work itself. Tracking manufacturing cost, for example, is comparably simple. You count up the materials used in production, add the labor of employees manning the production line, amortize the use of the equipment, and end up with a solid number. IT work, on the other hand, is a lot more ephemeral. How do you account for innumerable bytes of code generated by IT developers or for the myriad small tasks that go into managing daily IT operations?

For this, IT needs processes and tools that support activity-based costing (ABC). This costing model can be used to help identify all the activities that go into providing an IT service. IT can account for both direct and indirect cost, and thus better evaluate the overall cost associated with a specific service or process such as employee onboarding.

Fortunately, the ITIL framework defines a library of standard IT activities which saves you the work of defining them for yourself and comparing your definitions to those of your competitors. Using ITIL, your IT organization can quickly pinpoint the activities that go into the most significant services delivered to the business.

It is important, however, to resist the temptation to boil the ocean. While knowledge is power, IT does not need to know everything about everything it does – at least not in the beginning. It's best to target a high-value service at first, and apply an ABC accounting methodology to gain insight into the activities involved for the service, as in the employee onboarding example.

Based on such an approach, IT can gain more insight into costs and performance, and use this information to arrive at informed make-or-buy decisions. For instance, would it make business sense to invest money to streamline the employee onboarding process, or would it be better to simply outsource the process to a specialist provider? Alternatively, such insight might show that IT performs well above the industry norm – in which case IT can use this information to remind the business of its ongoing value.

Keep in mind, however, that to run itself as a business, IT must make decisions not only in terms of cost and performance but also with an eye to proper IT governance and effective management of risk. Unfortunately, most IT organizations carry out their risk management duties using spreadsheet-based manual methods, often spending weeks testing controls and compiling lists of deficiencies. Such lists can include hundreds of items, which makes it difficult to prioritize remediation efforts. And without a central repository for storing controls, organizations often lose track over which controls have been tested and which have not. This leads to duplicate controls and costly duplication of effort.

To address these challenges, many organizations are moving toward a continuous audit methodology for managing IT risk. Here, controls are consolidated to address multiple compliance requirements, and automated monitors are used to track IT controls and risk indicators in real time. Before predefined risk thresholds are exceeded, these monitors indicate the severity of the threat so that IT can effectively prioritize its response activities.

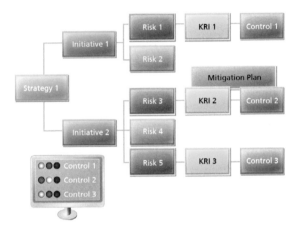

Figure 2.3 From business strategy to risks and risk controls

As Figure 2.3 shows, this automated approach to risk and control monitoring fits into an overall process that starts with strategy management for the entire business, including IT. First, the organization articulates its strategy and identifies initiatives and projects designed to execute on it. For instance, initiative 1 may be a data center consolidation project. Common risks for such a project would be widespread, from technological to legal to external and beyond:

- Have you made the right technical decisions?
- Are you legally allowed to store certain data, like human resources (HR), outside of the country?
- Are the chosen vendors liable and financially sound (which is harder to judge if you are dealing with new vendors in a new region)?

After rating and ranking all risks, you want to define key risk indicators (KRIs). Finally, automatic controls for the KRIs are defined and implemented. Ongoing data collection and comparison against these controls will keep your overall risk exposure under control. And in case a risk materializes, you can quickly leverage the defined mitigation plan and respond in a timely fashion.

Importantly, these controls need to be aligned with strategy so that the organization can take on an appropriate level of risk. No IT organization wants to take reckless risks that put the business in jeopardy. On the other hand, calibrating controls to an excessive level of risk aversion can put the business at a competitive disadvantage. Thus, it is important to close the performance and risk management loop by making decisions and continuously monitoring performance in the context of business strategy.

Solutions for IT Strategy and Performance from the SAP BusinessObjects™ Portfolio

The solutions discussed below – mostly drawn from the SAP BusinessObjects™ solution portfolio – play a critical role in helping your IT organization strike the balance between maximizing IT's contribution to the business while controlling cost and risk. They enable IT to better integrate with key business goals and consequently become more strategic (see Figure 2.4).

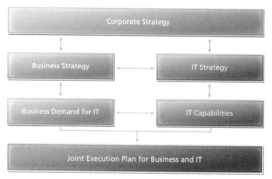

Figure 2.4 Business and IT goals derived from business strategy

SAP BusinessObjects Strategy Management

Business projects that are able to move forward without the involvement of IT are few and far between. This indicates the importance of integrating business strategy and IT strategy. To achieve this integration, IT organizations must ensure that their plans directly support the overall corporate strategy and that IT capabilities and initiatives support business demands. When planning is collaborative, the resulting joint execution plan for business and IT will help ensure the organization is aiming in a single direction.

The plan should identify the key performance indicators used to measure the performance of the objectives. It is critical also to define the initiatives that must get done to achieve the objectives. Initiatives must be assigned owners and teams responsible for doing the work. Next, the plan should be clearly communicated, and then monitored closely to manage progress. At the same time, employees must be able to leverage tools to support them in their day-to-day tasks, as well as help them make well-informed decisions that can help improve performance and reduce risk.

The SAP BusinessObjects Strategy Management application can empower IT staff at all levels to rapidly align resources so that you can execute your business strategy better, understand risk better, and become more effective. By aligning IT plans with business plans, associating objectives, performance measures, initiatives and people, you can better prioritize IT staff and move forward with confidence and purpose.

Key features in SAP BusinessObjects Strategy Management include:

- **Communication tools such as strategy maps and scorecards based on the balanced scorecard methodology** that help you transform written plans into living documents that can then be used by employees to define, discuss, share, and manage the activities necessary to achieve goals

- **Collaboration tools** that help you motivate employees and encourage greater collaboration when analyzing performance issues – making relevant data available and capturing the analysis and supporting documents in context
- **Initiative management tools** that help you prioritize and deploy resources more efficiently by understanding interdependencies, "below horizon" objectives, and risks; they also help you identify key initiatives that must get done in order to achieve the strategic goals

Figure 2.5 IT Cockpit leveraging the balanced scorecard concept

These tools enable you to run IT like a business by helping you to:

- **Effectively manage and collaborate on strategy** within IT and, more importantly, with key stakeholders outside IT, and quickly assess strategic performance

- **Set clear IT priorities and communicate key initiatives** by focusing on the initiatives that will have the greatest impact and allocating resources appropriately
- **Gain clear visibility and accountability across the organization** by managing exceptions and ensuring that individuals understand how they can affect strategic goals

If you are able to adopt systematic strategy management processes within your company for both business and IT, and align business units and IT around common objectives, you will have taken a huge step toward maximizing performance. It will help blur the borders between the two teams, reducing the all-too-common business versus IT ("them versus us") mentality. And IT will be a big step closer to transforming the perception of being a reactive order taker, and will instead be seen as a proactive problem solver – something at which IT practitioners excel.

SAP BusinessObjects Profitability and Cost Management

Effectively organizing, navigating, and interpreting IT financial data requires the right costing approach and the right tool to support it. The SAP BusinessObjects Profitability and Cost Management application is a flexible and scalable software tool that features ready-to-use functionality for activity-based costing (ABC). As Figure 2.6 shows, ABC modeling lets you associate the various costs in your organization (properties, assets, people, capital, and technology) with the work they perform and the services, applications, and internal customers they underpin. This approach ultimately lets you more clearly visualize the cost of delivering a service, running an application, or serving a customer.

Business Services

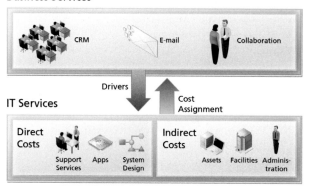

Figure 2.6 Costing approach with SAP® BusinessObjects™ Profitability and Cost Management

This model is orchestrated by SAP BusinessObjects Profitability and Cost Management, allowing you to quickly and clearly plot the true direct and indirect costs associated with your services, applications, and internal customers. The result is a clear view into the financial data required for fact-based IT business management.

Key features and benefits include:
- **A preformatted logical data structure** to speed implementation with minimal ongoing maintenance
- **Web-based data collection and built-in work management functionality** to allow IT staff to enter non-system driver data supported by reminders and automated alerts
- **Flexible costing methodologies** to allow you to choose the best costing approach for the situation
- **A wizard-driven rules engine** for easy modeling of complex business rules

- **Single-step multidimensional assignment** for more accurate costing with less chance of error
- **Comprehensive user-defined trace-back** to enable tracing activities back to the GL line-item expenses, providing the greatest possible cost transparency and traceability

SAP BusinessObjects Profitability and Cost Management helps you manage the business of IT by:

- Enabling better cost-justified IT investment decisions
- Driving more cost-effective use of IT capability
- Increasing the transparency and accuracy of IT costs
- Encouraging more informed and productive dialogue with business users about funding and IT service commitments
- Implementing equitable and supportable charging models

While the above concepts can be overwhelming at first, applying and leveraging them for key IT decisions or activities will drive understanding of the benefits and further broader adoption. And even if you and your company are not yet ready to make IT a profit center instead of a cost center, having insight into cost and performance data, comparing it to the external market, and educating the IT user on this data have been shown to drive a tremendous change in IT consumption behavior as well as IT recognition.

SAP BusinessObjects Spend Performance Management

IT spend takes a significant percentage of the overall company spend and covers a huge variety of items. Not managing this spend professionally often means not taking advantage of vendor consolidation or volume discounts, for example.

The SAP BusinessObjects Spend Performance Management application enables IT sourcing professionals to access timely and accurate data on what is being purchased, from which suppliers, and how much is being spent. This visibility helps you quickly and efficiently identify cost savings opportunities, rationalize suppliers, monitor compliance, track progress toward meeting goals, and manage overall spend performance.

Top 8 Suppliers

Supplier	Spend [USD]	% of Total Spend
Data Center Provider	10,103,829	7.2
Hardware Vendor	9,012,597	6.4
IT Equipment Unlimited	7,415,830	5.3
Global Telecom	6,814,329	4.8
North American Printing Company	6,570,918	4.7
Third-Party Outsourcing	5,601,483	4.0
Global Consulting	5,235,190	3.7
Business Automation	4,328,775	3.1

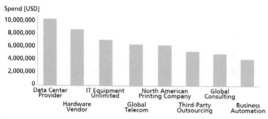

Figure 2.7 Lower IT cost through insight into spending pattern

Key features and benefits include:

- **Automated data capture** from disparate systems that helps you gain full spend visibility
- **Built-in analytics** to help you have a rapid impact on IT spend performance and show results
- **Built-in spend advisor functionality** to help you establish and monitor key performance indicators

SAP BusinessObjects Spend Performance Management helps you manage the business of IT by:

- Driving a shared view of spend performance
- Rapidly identifying and acting on savings opportunities
- Proactively monitoring contract compliance
- Identifying supply risks and prioritizing mitigation actions

With the size of the IT spend and today's cost-consciousness, neglecting IT spend management is like throwing money down the drain.

SAP BusinessObjects Risk Management

When IT plays such a critical role in business success, effective IT risk management is a vital business requirement. IT complexity and the fast pace of business itself, however, mean that manual, reactive risk management processes won't do. Organizations today need automated capabilities that support continuous auditing. This is what the SAP BusinessObjects Risk Management application supports.

Taking an end-to-end lifecycle approach, this application helps IT plan and scope key risks and controls in the context of business strategy. You can identify and document risks, key risk indicators, control objectives, and control test results. You can also analyze your control environment and take remediation steps for controls found to be ineffective. Continuous monitoring of key risk indicators and controls help ensure real-time insight into your overall risk profile and state of compliance. Response and mitigation functionality, meanwhile, help ensure speedy resolution when problems occur. Figure 2.8 shows the closed-loop model for SAP BusinessObjects Risk Management.

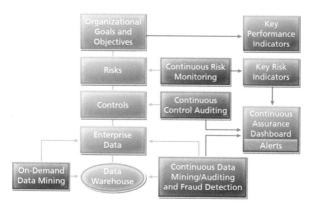

Figure 2.8 Continuous risk and control assurance model

Together, these functions help deliver automated, proactive risk and control monitoring and management across business processes, enabling you to understand the key risks and control issues for IT processes as they occur rather than after the fact. This helps minimize the cost of managing risks and controls across the entire compliance program.

Key features of SAP BusinessObjects Risk Management allow you to:
- Identify all key risks across the enterprise
- Drive agreement on top process risks and thresholds
- Perform qualitative and quantitative risk analysis
- Create control mitigation strategies that maximize return on capital
- Build proactive control monitoring into existing business processes
- Document new compliance initiatives using a top-down risk-based approach
- Automate risk and control monitoring processes
- Analyze issues, perform necessary remediation and certify results

Any company that has ever experienced the financial and reputational implications of theoretical risks that became reality understands the need for risk management. All other companies can either take note and start to proactively manage risk or learn the hard way.

Identity Management and Access Control

Identity management and system access control are among the most traditional duties for any IT organization, and are still highly relevant. Without a workable approach to both, businesses cannot expect to maintain data confidentiality and enforce policies related to the segregation of duties. And without an automated approach to both, IT cannot expect to keep up with the tasks required to manage them.

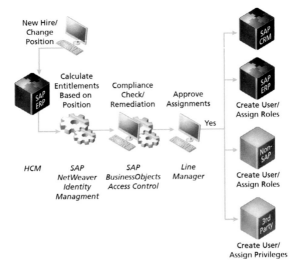

Figure 2.9 Combined solutions for identity management and access control

SAP offers two solutions that work separately or together to help you manage these tasks. These are the SAP NetWeaver® Identity Management (SAP NetWeaver ID Management) component and the SAP BusinessObjects Access Control application.

SAP NetWeaver Identity Management

SAP NetWeaver ID Management helps you manage users' access to applications securely and efficiently, while meeting audit and compliance requirements. Providing a central mechanism for provisioning users in accordance with their current business roles, this component works with all your systems and applications – not just your SAP software. It also supports related processes such as password management, self-service, and approvals workflow.

Key features of SAP NetWeaver Identity Management include:

- **Identity virtualization** to provide an integrated, unified view of users' virtual identities and to let you leverage information and access right across networks
- **Data synchronization** to propagate key information from one application to other related applications to maintain data consistency and quality
- **Provisioning, workflow, and approvals** to help ensure prompt, fully auditable, policy-driven assignment and maintenance of user access rights across multiple systems
- **Password management** to allow self-service updates and synchronization of passwords and personal information, reducing the workload of your service desk staff
- **Roles and entitlements** to align user rights and privileges with the roles performed in business processes, not a technical directory structure
- **Reporting and auditing** to enable transparency and conclusive documentation on current access and past events

SAP BusinessObjects Access Control

SAP BusinessObjects Access Control enables all corporate compliance stakeholders – including business managers, auditors, and IT security managers – to collaboratively and continuously control access and authorizations to assets across the enterprise and help ensure segregation of duties (SoD) compliance.

The software unifies SoD and access risk analysis and remediation, enterprise role management, compliant user provisioning, emergency privilege management, and privilege attestation and provides a holistic, enterprise-wide view in real time. It can help you ensure day-to-day compliance, provide comprehensive management oversight, and perform effective and complete audits. As a result, you can improve your ability to protect information and prevent fraud while minimizing the time and cost associated with compliance processes.

Key features of SAP BusinessObjects Access Control include:

- **Access control and authorization** to help you enforce SoD compliance with role design, documentation, and maintenance that prevents improper access to assets, automatically eliminates access and authorization risks, and enforces best practices
- **Automated compliance** to help you automate end-to-end processes and reduce audit-related costs for access and authorization risk detection, remediation, and mitigation
- **Real-time reporting** that enables you to oversee and predict compliance, prevent security and controls violations, and provide for faster resolution of issues

Used in conjunction with one another, SAP NetWeaver ID Management and SAP BusinessObjects Access Control allow you to perform risk validation before users are provisioned. Here, SAP NetWeaver ID Management can perform provisioning checks and associated tasks for multiple target systems running SAP BusinessObjects Access Control to help ensure proper SoD. This can be highly advantageous in fast-moving environments where users switch roles on a regular basis.

For example, let's say an existing employee in the accounting department has access to the accounts payable system. After several years with the company, this employee moves over to the procurement department and finds herself in charge of buying core materials used in the manufacture of the company's goods. This requires new access to new systems and new data. As this access is requested, a system using SAP NetWeaver ID Management and SAP BusinessObjects Access Control in conjunction can automatically check the user provisioning request against SoD. Policies or regulations, for instance, may aim to build a wall between roles that allow procurement authority and those that issue payments for procured items.

If this conflict were not caught, the company would expose itself to the risk of potential fraudulent activities as well as violations that might be uncovered during an audit. Using the 'detect and prevent' functions of SAP NetWeaver ID Management and SAP BusinessObjects Access Control, your IT group can catch conflicts like this in real time. In such a case, the software would send an alert to the appropriate parties to indicate that a decision needs to be made – which, in this scenario, would most likely result in the revocation of access right for the systems required to carry out the duties of the previous role. In the end, this enables IT to help the company minimize risk and remain in compliance with existing policies and regulations, therefore increasing the business value of IT.

Services for IT Strategy and Performance from SAP

Most companies are fully aware of the need to better manage IT performance and governance. But where and how to start? SAP can help here too.

SAP provides premium consulting services to help you develop and maintain IT as a strategic resource within your organization. Our consulting groups possess strong IT knowledge as well as solid business acumen, a combination that is essential when introducing and evolving tools and tactics for measuring and managing IT performance in business terms.

Enterprise Performance Management Services

SAP consultants help translate business and IT strategy into operational objectives and metrics that drive and measure IT performance in business-oriented terms. Leveraging the SAP BusinessObjects enterprise performance management (EPM) solutions, EPM consultants help you:

- Define strategy and prioritize activities for integrating your IT and business goals
- Plan, budget, forecast, and allocate resources in line with organizational constraints
- Model and optimize IT cost drivers
- Apply comprehensive, relevant, and flexible analytics

The result is greater transparency into IT performance, better visibility into business drivers and how they affect IT, and an IT organization better positioned to deliver on business priorities as they evolve over time.

Business Transformation Services

The Business Transformation Services group of SAP Consulting provides a range of services, from strategy through execution, to connect your business and IT and maximize returns on your IT investment and optimize processes organization-wide. This service portfolio features:

- **SAP Value Partnership services** to help you create measurable value through business transformation
- **Business clarity services** to help you gain insight into the performance of your business and IT for improved joint planning and decision making
- **Business impact services** to help you realize optimized business processes and organizational efficiency with a business-driven IT architecture

The Business Transformation Services group employs a flexible and collaborative approach aimed at delivering optimum value quickly and efficiently. Services can be delivered on an advisory, consulting project, or long-term partner basis. Beyond the expertise of the group's consultants, you also benefit from the group's continuously upgraded business process library featuring best practices developed in collaboration with SAP customers, as well as over 3,500 benchmark case studies and 1,000 business cases.

Business transformation services help you manage the business of IT by:

- Improving IT relevance by enabling your IT organization to grow beyond its role as a technology service provider into a fully-fledged partner to the enterprise
- Increasing return on investment (ROI) through innovative and creative concepts delivered by our expert consultants
- Improving operational performance by optimizing business processes based on best practices and by enhancing process governance
- Lowering the total cost of ownership and freeing additional budget for innovation by enhancing your IT strategy and landscape and effectively managing your SAP investment

2.3 IT Portfolio and Project Management

The days are long gone when IT could impress the business by simply delivering IT projects that are on time and on budget. Today, businesses assume this level of service and are looking for much more – namely, value. IT is under great pressure to pick and choose the right projects – among a mass of possibilities – that will deliver the greatest value to the business. Here, value is measured both in terms of ROI and the ability to advance the strategic business objectives.

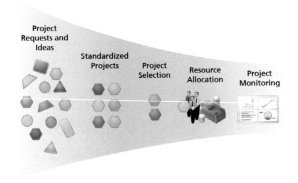

Figure 2.10 Well-managed project selection funnel

The key for IT is to evaluate all potential projects from a portfolio perspective, using a disciplined methodology (similar to the project funnel shown in Figure 2.10) to run through what-if scenarios and assess value based on solid business criteria.

In the end, the projects that IT chooses must address business priorities. Unfortunately, IT often finds itself out of the loop when it comes to the specifics of corporate strategy, which makes it difficult to understand business priorities and line up projects designed to address them.

To serve the business more effectively, IT needs to get closer to the origination of business strategy. The role of the CIO, when it is elevated to executive board status, goes a long way toward addressing this issue. Solutions such as SAP BusinessObjects Strategy Management (discussed in the previous section) can then take the priorities of the business and manage them in a rationalized manner to help ensure that IT aligns its activities with overall corporate strategy.

It is also important for IT to focus on the issue of resource constraints. Let's say an automobile manufacturer builds 60 percent of its vehicles for the low-end, entry-level market in emerging economies. It also builds 25 percent of its vehicles for the mid-market in North America, and 15 percent for the high-end luxury market in Europe. Will an IT project aimed at supporting the dealership network in China make more sense than a project focused on improving supply chain collaboration in North America and Europe?

While strategic considerations are important here, IT must also weigh the value of each project based on an analysis of the resource demands involved. Such an analysis may show that developing a Chinese dealership network would be a praiseworthy long-term goal, but that the resource demands would be prohibitive – in which case the business may wish to consider modifying the plan or dropping it all together.

Though this example is certainly oversimplified, the point is that IT must conduct a clear cost-benefit analysis. This is what it means for IT to run itself as a business, and this is also what will engender respect from the larger organization that IT serves.

At the same time, IT should be wary of using the issue of resource constraints as an excuse for not moving forward with strategically important initiatives. Wherever possible, IT must take steps to free up the resource bottlenecks that commonly occur in any IT organization so that the business can do more. This means breaking loose of the traditionally siloed structure of IT and leveraging resources wherever they may exist. When it comes to human resources, this requires IT to get far more comfortable with collaboration. It also requires solutions that help identify where you may be able to find the talent required for your project. At a time when IT staff members are seldom assembled under one roof, this challenge requires human capital management software tools that can track skills and help IT managers quickly identify the right person for the job.

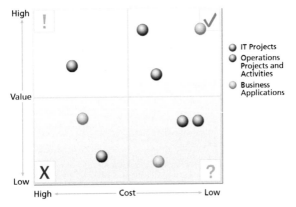

Figure 2.11 Portfolio evaluation across various IT concerns

In the context of all these challenges, portfolio and project planning calls for tools that are both proactive and reactive. On the proactive side, you need the ability to understand business strategy, associate it with the pool of available projects, and run projections that help you assess ROI and ultimate value based on solid financial metrics that can be clearly communicated to the business. Figure 2.11 shows this concept consistently applied for large projects and smaller activities, as well as business applications.

On the reactive side, you need tools that help increase IT controls, enabling you to continuously monitor your portfolio of projects and measure risk exposure as projects progress through the lifecycle. This level of control will also give you the ability to respond to sudden changes that affect IT funding – whether the changes are specific to your company or stem from larger economic conditions that are largely out of your control. If your IT budget is cut, for example, how would the cuts affect the business? Would the cost savings outweigh the reduced business benefit? Having answers to these kinds of questions may influence the CFO to reconsider the proposed budget cut.

Having systematic what-if capabilities that are able to balance IT supply and demand in a closed-loop iterative cycle, as shown in Figure 2.12, will make your IT department much more agile and accountable for its priorities and decisions. At all times, you can show and explain the underlying data to your IT decisions.

The solution discussed next supports these capabilities: the SAP Portfolio and Project Management application.

Figure 2.12 Dynamic optimization of IT supply and demand

SAP Portfolio and Project Management

SAP Portfolio and Project Management is designed to help you deliver business value through your IT portfolio. It includes the former SAP Resource and Portfolio Management application and Collaboration Projects application, which have been reconciled under the new name. SAP Portfolio and Project Management enables effective management at three levels – portfolio, project, and operations – to help you align your IT organization's activities and resources with business priorities.

Figure 2.13 Complete approach used in SAP Portfolio and Project Management

SAP Portfolio and Project Management lets you systematically gather project requests and ideas. You can then apply standard project templates and scoring schemes to assess priority. Resources can be assigned and progress monitored throughout execution.

SAP Portfolio and Project Management gives you essential visibility into your entire project portfolio, allowing you to monitor the progress of all your project and operations activities. Its sophisticated portfolio management functions let you control the key stages of every project lifecycle. With SAP Portfolio and Project Management, you can:

- Identify and prioritize worthwhile initiatives, projects, and project proposals
- Set priorities

- Select the most suitable employees or contractors for each project
- Monitor and coordinate project activities and resources

The clear visibility and control that SAP Portfolio and Project Management provides helps you minimize risk and optimize labor and financial resources, even as requirements, metrics, resources, and schedules change. As a result, you can keep timelines on target, budgets in check, and team members better informed.

SAP Portfolio and Project Management integrates well with existing heterogeneous IT landscapes and leverages data from disparate systems such as HR, financial, project management, and desktop systems. This enables new, cross-functional business processes and provides ready insight into operations.

Key portfolio management features include:

- **Dashboards** to provide a concise view of initiative, project, proposal, and operational service status and performance against key indicators
- **Decision support** to help you identify, monitor, and trend your key decision-making criteria across the portfolio, highlighting underperforming projects and operations
- **Financial planning** with granular measures to display and monitor time-based costs and benefits to ensure attainment of anticipated results
- **Integration with HR software and long-range resource planning** to help you best position your workforce to meet future needs
- **Questionnaires and risk assessment** that feed scoring models to support portfolio evaluation and resource allocation
- **Gate and portfolio reviews** to drive decision making around budgeting, resources, and scheduling
- **What-if analysis** to help you view your portfolio within different scenarios and evaluate the impact of critical changes

- **Virtual collaboration rooms** including automated notifications to enable project participants to chat, collaborate on documents, and view project calendars and risk status
- **Evaluation models and sophisticated analytics** to help compare quantitative and qualitative metrics and produce ranked lists of projects, proposals, resource utilization, and baseline services

SAP Portfolio and Project Management helps you manage the business of IT by:

- Enabling IT to focus on key projects and activities
- Decreasing implementation time for new IT capability
- Streamlining the capture and assessment of new requests and proposals
- Enriching the gate review process and reducing the administration associated with regular portfolio, program, and project reviews
- Aligning the IT portfolio more closely with corporate objectives
- Identifying risk early and monitoring it methodically throughout the project lifecycle

Using SAP Portfolio and Project Management is a significant step toward making your IT supply chain transparent and predictable – a significant part of running your IT department as a business.

Services for Portfolio and Project Management from SAP

For most SAP solutions, the demand for services and the services required vary dramatically from region to region. This is why we offer a mix of services that are delivered by SAP Consulting or one of our many certified service partners.

Wherever your IT organization stands along the portfolio and project management maturity curve, SAP Consulting or one of its partners can help you plan, build, and run your implementation of SAP Portfolio and Project Management to maximize the value of your investment and improve IT effectiveness. Our consultants can quickly get you up to speed on the challenges you and your business face, and develop a cost-effective project plan, whether you're executing an upgrade, implementing targeted functionality, or deploying the full solution for the first time.

Once the plan is approved, we can then marshal the resources required to implement the solution in a way that minimizes project costs and the risk of business disruption. We can even help you run your solution with an eye toward incremental improvements to maximize the value of your investment over time and minimize your total cost of ownership.

While SAP Consulting offers these services in many regions, SAP partners are also used to gain maximum coverage while delivering the same level of service. Two partners of note include:

- Penitus Global Solutions (www.penitus.com)
- Platinum DB Consulting (www.platinumdb.com)

2.4 IT Service Management

More than anything else, the IT service desk acts as the
face of IT to the customer – whether the customer is
external or an internal end user. Ideally, IT would like to put its best foot
forward when any customer calls in with an issue (see Figure 2.14).

Unfortunately, many IT organizations lack standardized service desk
processes. They often struggle against service desk sprawl, as individual
domains set up separate service desk operations to manage their own silos
in isolation. The result can be frustration on the part of customers who
find it difficult to get straight answers to resolve issues as they arise.

Figure 2.14 The Service Desk as IT's face to the customer

To avoid this frustration and to run itself more effectively as a business, IT must consolidate service desk functionality throughout the enterprise and manage processes in a consistent manner according to the widely accepted standards articulated in ITIL V3. The aim is to establish a single IT service management (ITSM) process and a single point of access for all incidents and problems. With all calls related to IT performance flowing into one service desk console, and a clear process in place to achieve resolution, IT management can better align its activities with business priorities and evaluate performance in the context of service-level agreements.

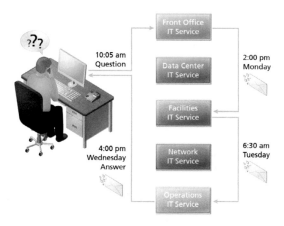

Figure 2.15 Lack of IT process integration – too often the status quo

While many vendors support a single, standardized process for ITSM, most of them approach the market with a history of building and delivering technical tools. SAP, on the other hand, stands apart as an undisputed leader in the area of process innovation. What's more, SAP offers its solution for ITSM as a fully integrated part of the SAP CRM application. This means that the solution you use for incident, problem, and change management is part and parcel of the SAP Business Suite applications that your IT organization already manages. This level of integration is simply unachievable by tool vendors who come at ITSM from a less process-oriented starting point.

Consider too that SAP CRM is widely recognized as one of the premier applications for effective customer management and interaction. For an IT organization seeking to run itself as a business, what can be more important than clear, proven process support that helps ensure a consistently positive experience for the customers it serves?

Standardized processes and integrated tools, in turn, lay a firm foundation for automation and improved reporting. Automated workflow, for example, can trigger scripts to run that can resolve common problems without the intervention of an IT engineer. On the reporting side, IT can quickly identify groups of incidents that may be related to a common root cause. A single problem logged against these incidents can then be sent to an engineer for resolution. In the long run, both of these scenarios can help alleviate demand on front-line support agents and allow more highly paid engineers to focus their energies on higher-value activities.

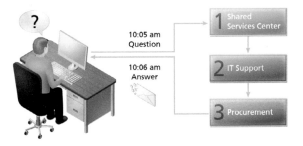

Figure 2.16 Integrated IT service management process

The ultimate goal is a complete end-to-end ITSM process that integrates the initial report of an issue with the logistics and execution processes required to resolve it. Let's say an IT service desk agent receives a stream of calls from end users complaining about a slow web-based application. These incidents are quickly grouped and assigned to a single problem record, which is assigned to an engineer. The problem is traced to a network router crash that forces network traffic to an alternate gateway, which in turn has an adverse impact on the performance of the application in question. The engineer quickly researches the router history and finds that it is due for replacement within the next two months. He then weighs this replacement information against historical repair cost data and decides to replace the router then and there, two months ahead of schedule. He creates a request for change and – after the request is approved – launches the purchase order for the new router directly from the change request, attaching his rationale for auditing purposes. Once the router arrives, he makes the replacement and closes out the problem and all related documents.

With the SAP IT Service Management (SAP ITSM) application, described below, IT organizations can manage the entire ITSM process. This helps make IT more efficient and more responsive to the needs of the business.

SAP IT Service Management

SAP IT Service Management helps you implement and automate IT service management best practices such as ITIL in an end-to-end fashion. Integrated business scenarios such as the router example above can be successfully modeled with SAP ITSM using its innate integration within the SAP Business Suite. SAP ITSM helps you define, manage, and optimize essential ITIL-verified service management processes as shown in Figure 2.17 and connect them to your standard logistics and finance processes via SAP Business Suite.

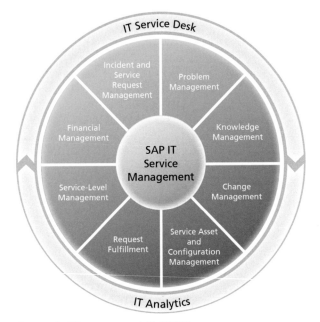

Figure 2.17 Key ITIL processes supported by SAP ITSM

Key features of SAP IT Service Management include:

- **Service-level management**, allowing you to define and manage all IT services, their related service-level agreements (SLAs) and contracts, and allocate costs appropriately
- **Incident and service request management**, supporting prompt, efficient resolution of user issues and requests through systematic capture, documentation, and tracking
- **Problem management**, helping to prevent recurrent issues by facilitating investigation, resolution, and documentation of errors and corresponding workarounds or solutions

- **Change management**, helping maximize the effectiveness of your entire change process through comprehensive control of requests, approval, and documentation
- **Knowledge management**, speeding issue resolution and reducing recurrence by centralizing key information in a central repository searchable by support analysts and end users
- **Installed-base and object management**, an integrated configuration management system that helps you track and manage the configuration items relied on in service processes
- **IT analytics**, providing valuable insight into IT service processes and performance through concise reporting and built-in analytics (see Figure 2.18)

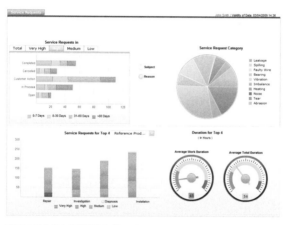

Figure 2.18 Built-In SAP ITSM Dashboard

Key features of SAP ITSM include:

- **Preconfigured, best practice–based functionality** to help you reduce implementation time and more quickly realize results
- **Automatic assignment and escalation** based on business rules, priorities, and service level agreements (SLAs) to help you accelerate incident and problem resolution
- **SLA-based prioritization and categorization** to optimize service desk workload management
- **Automated change approval workflow** to help you ensure prompt, positive approval of all changes
- **An integrated, centralized knowledge base** to improve knowledge capture and reuse, driving quicker, more efficient incident and problem resolution
- **A built-in integration interface to SAP Solution Manager** to enable faster resolution of application-related incidents
- **Built-in integration with the SAP ERP Financials solution** to help you make better decisions through better insight into cost
- **Powerful, built-in analytics** to provide meaningful analysis of support and operational performance from day one

SAP ITSM helps you manage the business of IT by:

- Increasing IT service quality and transparency through standardizing and automating IT processes
- Cutting delivery costs through streamlined support and change management processes
- Coordinating IT priorities and budget with IT operations by integrating cost information and asset management functionality available in SAP ERP
- Clearly defining expectations and managing performance according to SLAs

Services for IT Service Management from SAP

There is a vast array of SAP services as well as certified solution partner services for the SAP Business Suite. Additionally, SAP offers rapid deployment of the SAP IT Service Desk Operation application, which helps ensure the speed and success of your deployment at a fixed price. Rapid deployment of this and other solutions is further described in the section "Solution Enablers."

2.5 Application Lifecycle Management

The primary reason for running IT as a business is to enable IT to deliver greater value to the larger business it serves. And when it comes to delivering value to the business, applications are where the rubber hits the road.

Infrastructure components remain critically important for IT – but if IT is doing its job correctly, nobody on the business side of the organization ever needs to lay hands on a server or a network router. Applications are different because they execute the front-end and back-end processes that companies use to differentiate themselves in the market. Equally important for IT is the fact that business users experience applications in a direct way on a day-to-day basis. On the most practical level, applications serve as the most common touch point between the business and IT. Thus, when the business has a problem with an application, it has a problem with IT. This makes proper Application Lifecycle Management (ALM) extremely important to any IT organization seeking to demonstrate its value to the business.

Figure 2.19 Cultural gap between IT teams

Unfortunately, ALM is often approached with a design-time bias that puts the emphasis on the steps required to build and implement an application. Little attention is given to what happens after the application goes live, which is where most of the value is delivered to the business. As the saying goes, the implementation team gets the party, and the operations team gets the hangover.

The SAP approach to ALM bridges the gap between implementation and operations to help IT deliver continuous value to the business (see Figures 2.19 and 2.20). After all, what use is it to build an application that doesn't work well in runtime? The goal of this end-to-end approach to ALM is to forge bonds and enable the sharing of information across the two phases of the application lifecycle. This creates synergies for the design/implementation team and the operations team, helping to improve performance on both sides. The operations team gains insight into the rationale behind the decisions made during the design phase, making it easier to resolve any issues that may arise. The design team gets feedback from operations, which helps to hone application builds in a cycle of continuous improvement. The result is that the business experiences fewer outages and performance issues over the long term, and IT gains a reputation for delivering high-quality services that meet or exceed business expectations.

Figure 2.20 SAP approach to ALM bridges gaps within IT teams

The SAP Approach to Application Lifecycle Management

SAP has developed a holistic, integrated approach to ALM based on ITIL. Leveraging SAP Solution Manager, this approach includes process support, specific tools, best practices, and services to manage SAP and non-SAP solutions throughout the complete application lifecycle. It also supports streamlined integration of third-party service management solutions.

This disciplined approach to managing the application lifecycle helps you implement high-quality solutions faster and operate them at lower cost, so that you can:

- Identify prioritized business requirements
- Map these prioritized requirements to existing or new application processes and functionality
- Blueprint, configure, and test the processes to be implemented or improved
- Define business-oriented KPIs and associated monitoring

Figure 2.21 shows the complete ALM offering from SAP.

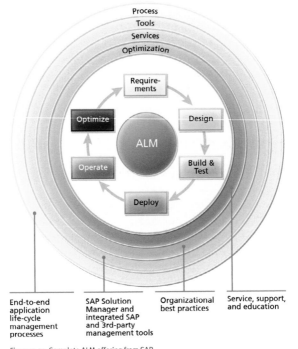

Figure 2.21 Complete ALM offering from SAP

All of this aims at a structured, comprehensive, unified, and reliable collection of information about all projects in progress and the state of the productive SAP solutions – what SAP calls the "single source of truth." This clarity is vital for making informed and fact-based decisions about your business solutions. With it, you can efficiently define and deploy the processes, responsibilities, SLAs, and KPIs necessary to deliver business value with SAP solutions.

Figure 2.22 Application Lifecycle Management with SAP

As Figure 2.22 shows, SAP Solution Manager serves as the technology platform for end-to-end ALM. Other key components for the SAP approach to ALM include:

- **ALM processes** that specify best practices and basic operational activities for the application lifecycle
- **Run SAP methodology** (discussed in detail in the "Solution Enablers" section), which supports the implementation of end-to-end solution operations and includes:
  - **The SAP standards for solution operations** – defined standards for key operations processes in business and IT

- **Road maps for the Run SAP methodology** – guidance on scoping, planning, setting up, and running an SAP solution
- **Best practices for the Run SAP methodology** – prototypes, guidance, and documented knowledge on industry- and function-specific business processes
- **Customer Center of Expertise (COE) organizations**, which follow the organizational model that drives integrated IT management
- **SAP Solution Manager**, the technology platform to support end-to-end solution operations

Application Lifecycle Management Processes

In contrast to typical ALM approaches illustrated on the left in Figure 2.23, SAP's approach is executed through processes spanning the complete application lifecycle (shown on the right). These range from requirements to operations and optimizations that enable accelerated innovation and reduced total cost of ownership while ensuring stable operation.

SAP provides ten best-practice processes for ALM to support both projects and solutions throughout the entire lifecycle:

- **Solution documentation** centrally documents and relates the business processes and technical information from SAP and non-SAP solutions to help ensure transparency, efficient maintenance, and collaboration
- **Solution implementation** identifies, adapts, and implements new and enhanced future-proof business and technical scenarios
- **Template management** allows customers with multisite SAP installations to manage their business processes efficiently across geographical distances
- **Test management** defines the integration testing requirements and test scope based on a change impact risk analysis; it is used to develop automatic and manual test cases, manage the testers, and report on the test progress and test results

Point Solutions	Integrated, ITIL-Oriented ALM
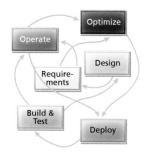	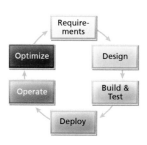

- ▪ Requires manual integration and/or customer integration
- ▪ Disparate and not consistent information for the entire lifecycle
- ▪ Hinders collaboration between phases and between business and IT
- ▪ Process gaps and disruptions

- ▪ Process continuity and consistency between each phase
- ▪ Improved visibility and transparency
- ▪ Better collaboration between distributed IT (dev./ops.), business, and partner teams
- ▪ Leverages ITIL best practices

Figure 2.23 Tackling the challenge of ALM point solutions

- **Change control management** drives workflow-based management of business- and technology-driven solution improvement changes with integrated project management, quality management, and synchronized deployment capabilities
- **Application incident management** enables centralized and common incident and issue message processing on multiple organization levels: it offers a communication channel with all relevant incident stakeholders and provides tight integration with SAP ITSM
- **Technical operations** represent all functionality for monitoring, alerting, analysis, and administration of SAP solutions
- **Business process operations** comprise the most important application-related operations necessary to ensure the smooth and reliable flow of the core business processes to meet a company's business requirements

- **Maintenance management** covers software correction packages, from discovery and retrieval to test scope optimization, possibly including optional automatic deployment into the production environment
- **Upgrade management** identifies, adapts, and implements new and enhanced business and technical scenarios, and uses SAP Solution Manager to manage the upgrade project holistically end-to-end

These defined functions allow faster implementation of the essential processes needed to optimize application reliability and reduce costs.

Customer Center of Expertise (COE)

Your single source of truth drives fact-based decision-making and relies heavily on an integrated IT and quality management process across all business and IT units. Unsatisfactory IT and quality management inhibits the efficiency of operations and responsiveness to business demands.

The Customer COE shown in Figure 2.24 is a facilitative organization that helps implement, monitor, and enforce integrated quality management using ALM processes, methodologies, and tools. This team acts across business units to bring stakeholders to the table to resolve challenges and issues. It helps manage mission-critical activities, providing:

- Accelerated innovation and investment protection
- Business continuity at a lower total cost of operations
- Business process improvement
- Successful integration of new business requirements

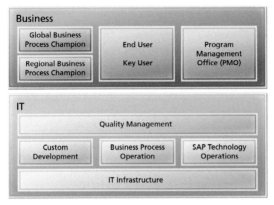

Figure 2.24 Proposed structure for a Customer Center of Expertise

The team also manages quality gates and helps to ensure that innovation is drawn directly from SAP to avoid unnecessary modification.

The roles of the Customer COE focus on safeguarding implementation projects, business continuity, business process improvement, and protection of investment. The Customer COE helps stimulate innovation by supporting processes that help you:

- Keep pace with changing business requirements
- Improve efficiency by advancing the general use of common methodologies throughout the company
- Improve development effectiveness through change management and quality testing
- Increase flexibility through adoption of service-oriented principles and easier integration of third-party solutions

SAP Solution Manager

SAP Solution Manager is the foundation of the SAP approach to application lifecycle management. The extensible platform provides a robust, centralized repository for an end-to-end approach to ALM that combines technical support for distributed systems with functionality that covers all key aspects of solution deployment, operation, and continuous improvement. Providing tools, content, and direct access to the applications and components within your IT landscape, SAP Solution Manager helps to increase the reliability of solutions and lower total cost of ownership.

With SAP Solution Manager, you can be sure that your entire SAP solution environment is performing at its maximum potential. The toolset addresses your entire IT environment, supporting SAP and non-SAP software and covering current and future SAP solutions. And, as a customer of SAP, you have access to the core SAP Solution Manager according to your support engagement at no extra charge.

SAP Solution Manager targets both technical and business aspects of your solutions, focusing strongly on core business processes. It supports the connection between business processes and the underlying IT infrastructure. As a result, it eases communication between your IT department and your lines of business. And it helps ensure that you derive the maximum benefits from your IT investments.

SAP Solution Manager provides the functionality needed to automate the ten ALM best-practice processes described earlier. Focusing on business solutions and IT projects, it supports both throughout their entire lifecycle.

SAP Solution Manager helps you manage the business of IT by:

- Accelerating conceptual design and configuration
- Streamlining testing and change management
- Supporting and optimizing end-to-end solution operations
- Providing consistent quality management processes across all technology stacks, code bases for the entire SAP platform and beyond
- Managing the fast pace of innovation and integration and the total cost of operations
- Improving compliance and reducing downtime
- Protecting your investment while stimulating innovation

Services for ALM from SAP

The services that SAP offers for application lifecycle management are rooted in almost 40 years of practical experience building and running critical business applications for the world's top companies. Our application management experts deliver proven best practices to optimize applications, simplify the IT landscape, and manage applications effectively through their entire lifecycle, thus allowing you to focus your resources on innovation and customer-facing activities.

SAP Enterprise Support

SAP Enterprise Support services help you respond rapidly to changing business needs through specialized expertise when it's needed. This support option offers:

- Access to the latest SAP software, enhancement packages, support and legal change packages, tools, and procedures
- Mission-critical support including 24x7 access to the SAP support advisory center and continuous quality checks to identify technical risks and optimization potential
- Global support backbone powered by SAP Solution Manager to help connect you with SAP experts and collaborate across an entire SAP ecosystem

- Access to valuable tools, standards, content, and communities focused on end-to-end solution operations
- Extended usage rights for SAP Solution Manager

SAP Enterprise Support provides you with the resources needed to manage complexity effectively and minimize risks in your SAP software environment. This enables your key resources to spend less time on maintenance and more time on innovation.

Services for Testing
Technology nonperformance and failure are expensive, potentially with severe financial or reputational consequences for the company. The criticality and complexity of IT systems and the increasing pressure to rapidly develop and deploy new applications and enhancements underscore the need for rigorous testing.

Testing is a complex process with many potential challenges, including tight timelines and potentially big decisions. Yet despite its make-or-break role, testing is frequently undervalued, inadequately scheduled, and unsatisfactorily managed. Further, many IT organizations lack the fundamental testing skills commensurate with the value of the applications being developed.

SAP recognizes the business value of comprehensive and effective testing of an IT landscape and offers proven methods and expert guidance to help you select and execute the right testing procedures in your environment. SAP consultants help you implement flexible, efficient, and replicable testing processes to verify the performance, security, and quality of your applications. From this, you can clearly identify and understand your IT landscape's strengths and weaknesses as well as its opportunities and threats.

Services for testing comprise a large portfolio featuring:

- Expert guidance in selecting the testing services that best address your IT and business requirements
- Strategy and assessment advisory services to develop the proper philosophy, practices, staff, and budget
- Test analysis and proof-of-concept services to implement the methodologies and tools needed to test business processes and applications
- Project management services for testing to assist you in managing testing projects and driving good software quality assurance practices
- Functional automation testing to support development of an effective automation methodology, tools, and reusable scripts
- Performance testing to validate application performance
- Environment management services to help you plan, implement, and operate test centers
- Training, education, and enablement services to provide skill and knowledge transfer from SAP testing experts to your staff

Services for testing provide you with the resources needed to deploy high-quality testing processes in your organization so you can achieve greater control of software costs and lower operational risk.

2.6 Infrastructure Management

Managing technology alone is not sufficient for IT
to create business value, but it is still a critical part of
running IT like a business. Infrastructure is the foundation of business
services and must be planned, managed, and optimized to achieve the
levels of reliability, availability, flexibility, and security dictated by business
needs.

As an enterprise software company, however, SAP does not focus its core
competencies on building the low-level tools that IT organizations require
for full infrastructure management. Nevertheless, SAP recognizes the
critical role that robust infrastructure management plays in the business
of IT. This is why, as part of the open ecosystem (see the "Ecosystem"
section), SAP is actively engaged with trusted partners such as Hewlett
Packard, CA, Novell, and Tidal Software to integrate their infrastructure
tools with SAP Solution Manager and other SAP software for managing
the business of IT.

In this context, SAP focuses more on the consumption of information
about the IT infrastructure than about the details of how each component
in the infrastructure is operating. Providing a consolidation layer for all the
different tools and technologies that exist across the layers of infrastructure,
SAP delivers high-level dashboards targeted toward IT management. The
goal is to monitor the relationship between technology components and
the services that IT delivers to the business from an end-user point of view.
Frequently, when a low-level drill-down is required, SAP relies on solution
extensions such as the SAP Extended Diagnostics application by CA Wily,
which powers low-level root cause analysis throughout the technology stack.

This application, and other tools from a growing list of partners, expresses
SAP's ongoing commitment to integrating its own software for running IT
as a business with the wide range of existing IT management tools available
on the market today.

Despite our emphasis on partnering in the lower-level IT management domain, SAP invests heavily in core emerging areas like virtualization, where the goal is to build a vertical integration from IT business management down to the virtualized IT components. While this is discussed in the final chapter in more detail, the following section focuses on one particular tool developed by SAP to help manage IT environments that use virtualization technology: the SAP NetWeaver Adaptive Computing Controller tool. Finally, we also discuss some of the services that SAP offers to help with infrastructure management.

SAP NetWeaver Adaptive Computing Controller Tool

Traditionally designed IT landscapes typically feature dedicated physical servers for business-critical applications. Calibrated to meet peak demand rather than average demand, these dedicated resources often use only a fraction of their full capacity, resulting in the major portion of hardware, power, and maintenance costs devoted to idling infrastructure.

Virtualization is a technology capable of liberating IT, allowing allocation of applications and data to servers and storage devices as computing

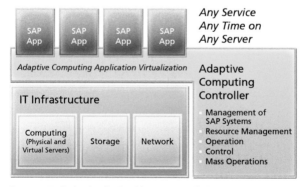

Figure 2.25 Application virtualization with SAP NetWeaver® Adaptive Computing Controller

demand and hardware availability fluctuates. This enables you to optimize utilization of your IT landscape, reducing complexity and constraints and providing significant opportunities for cost savings.

SAP NetWeaver Adaptive Computing Controller is a scalable virtualization tool that is part of a broad approach to self-managing dynamic systems. The Adaptive Computing Controller provides a central point of control for flexibly assigning computing resources to run any service on any server at any time. Figure 2.26 gives a glimpse at the highest level of the control and management consoles in this tool.

Figure 2.26 Easy-to-read virtualization console in SAP NetWeaver® Adaptive Computing Controller

The Adaptive Computing Controller features:
• Hardware and operating system provisioning to make it possible to readily add and remove computing resources with minimal administrative effort across a variety of operating systems and blade servers from leading vendors

- Data storage to manage and assign instances involving SAP applications to a dedicated computing resource, storing application data on a centralized storage system on the network
- Network provisioning to enable building connections between computing and storage resources, providing a transport layer for virtualization, and supporting different network topologies (for example, TCP/IP, iSCSI, and Fibre Channel)
- Adaptive computing control to let you centrally operate, observe, and manage an adaptive business solution using standard technologies, such as J2EE, XML, and CIM, and interfaces with SAP Solution Manager

The adaptive computing controller helps you manage the business of IT by:

- Lowering the cost of operations and reducing total cost of ownership
- Harmonizing and simplifying the cost of managing your IT landscape
- Responding to dynamically changing business needs without huge investments in computing resources
- Maintaining high service levels with lower budgets

Services for Infrastructure Management from SAP

SAP recognizes the vital role that IT infrastructure plays in business-driven IT and offers expert-led services to help you evolve SAP and non-SAP IT landscapes into agile, cost-efficient, service-oriented environments.

SAP IT Planning Services and the System Landscape Optimization Group

Some of the most exciting and challenging times in IT come during a major business shift. Examples include spinning off a division, being acquired, implementing a major financial reorganization, or simply being under tremendous pressure to reduce cost. And while all these business events are highly complex in themselves, the complexity rises even higher when you consider the related IT activities triggered by these business events. Selectively and safely identifying, separating, and migrating all data

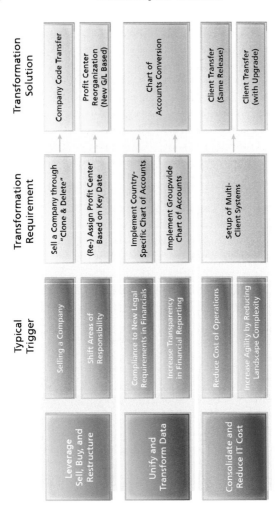

Figure 2.27 Business transformation's dependence on IT

belonging to a distinct division that is being sold is the closest thing IT has to open-heart surgery.

To address the typical customer business challenges shown in Figure 2.27, SAP offers a broad portfolio of IT planning and system landscape optimization services. Expert professionals with "surgical" SAP skills help you implement such changes within your SAP software landscape and beyond while maintaining business system and data integrity. Services can be delivered as needed, or SAP professionals can train your internal team to become self-reliant for future needs.

2.7   Solution Extensions from SAP

You are always looking for software that is optimized to meet your specific needs, can be implemented quickly, performs well, and offers minimal risk. SAP is always looking to provide you with innovative solutions that enhance the functionality and business value of SAP software.

Leveraging the resources of our growing ecosystem, SAP continually enlists the help of partners to produce powerful solution extensions. These partners are independent companies who develop software that integrates smoothly with SAP software and complements the comprehensive SAP solution portfolio, offering cross-industry and cross-solution functionality. To help ensure that the highest level of SAP quality is maintained, these partner-developed solutions are tested, validated, and approved by SAP development organizations and supported by the SAP community, providing the assurance of SAP quality, commitment, and support.

Solution extensions can help you:
• Increase the efficiency of end-to-end business processes for IT by improving visibility and enhancing reporting capabilities
• Optimize the use of existing IT resources
• Integrate SAP and non-SAP software processes
• Enhance software quality and reliability in customized, rapidly changing, and heterogeneous environments

While space prohibits listing all of the solution extensions available from SAP and its partners, the offerings mentioned below are particularly relevant for managing the business of IT. They are grouped according to the major IT management concerns discussed in this book, starting with the highest level of IT business management and progressing down the IT management stack.

IT Talent Visualization

If yours is like most IT organizations, your most valuable resource is your people. For any challenge you face – whether it's an immediate problem or a long-term strategic objective – you want to know who is who in your organization so that you can find the right people for the right job. This is even more important when the majority of your IT staff works overseas and you have never even met most of them face to face.

	Compare Competencies		
	Director of IT	Karen Miller	Paul Peterson
▲ Competencies Required by Position			
% Match			
Business Applications	Yes		
Databases	Outstanding		
Infrastructure	Very high		
IT Financial Management	High		
Business Process Analysis	Very high		
Project Management	Excellent		
▲ Other non-shared competencies possessed by Candidates (not required by position)			
Leadership skills		Very high	
Communication Skills		Above average	
Bachelor of Engineering		Without Rating	
Conceptual Thinking			Excellent
1.2 Event Organization			Low
1.3 Office General			Above average
2.1 Internal Accounting			Very high
2.2 External Accounting			Excellent
Knowledge in Economics			Very high
Certificate, Organizational Management			Above average
Enterprise Management			Very High

Figure 2.28 Succession planning with Talent Visualization

The SAP Talent Visualization application by Nakisa helps you meet this challenge by automating organizational charts. Fully web-based, this application leverages data in your existing SAP software environment, yielding greater visibility into organizational relationships and enabling improved HR data accuracy. Whenever someone in your IT group moves to a new position or leaves your company entirely, the change is automatically reflected in your organizational chart. This continually updated chart shows who reports to whom. This yields greater clarity into organizational roles and helps to facilitate collaboration throughout IT, whether your staff members sit in the next room or on an entirely different continent.

Equally important, SAP Talent Visualization helps you manage succession planning more effectively, so that you can continuously identify and develop new IT leaders. Providing real-time, in-depth visualization and execution of succession plans, the application helps you effectively align talent goals with your business strategies. Your ability to identify talent gaps and develop the talent pipeline improves, helping to ensure a powerful IT leadership strategy for the future. This creates a win-win situation by enhancing the organization's skills and offering a clear career path to key IT resources.

IT Project Insight

Because IT projects are so complex, it is often difficult to get a reliable reading of where you stand. The Crowdcast Collective Intelligence application can help. Though not formally an SAP solution extension, this application helps you to generate the project insight you need by leveraging your most valuable resource – your people. The idea is simple: decision makers within your IT group pose questions to project participants about key metrics and milestones – for example, "Will our supply network transformation project be completed on time and within budget?" Your co-workers, customers, or partners then bet on outcomes using virtual currency. Someone might bet that the project will be completed on time while predicting a budget overrun. Others with different perspectives and information may bet differently.

Respondents leave qualitative comments that provide the rationale behind their bets. The system aggregates all bets into a "crowdcast" – an accurate, unbiased prediction that incorporates the latest information in your extended organization. It also rewards accurate predictions and amplifies the voices of those who make them. In the end, decisions makers within your IT group gain real-time insight into otherwise inaccessible information about the status of key initiatives. This helps to keep projects on track and mitigate the risk of project delays.

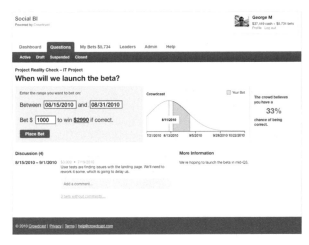

Figure 2.29 Tapping collective intelligence

Quality and Performance Testing

Running IT like a business means that you must constantly balance issues of cost and risk with an eye toward achieving the greatest possible value. Few areas of IT activity make this choice more evident than in quality and performance testing.

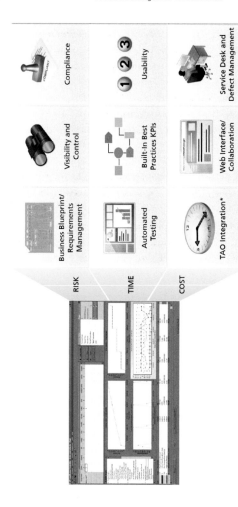

*TAO = Test Acceleration and Optimization

Figure 2.30   SAP Solution Manager with SAP Quality Center by HP

On one hand, you want to test new software releases to ensure the highest possible quality. After all, high-quality software that performs well under all conditions has a direct bearing on customer and end-user satisfaction.

On the other hand, you never want to be held hostage to onerous testing regimes, especially when more and more testing yields fewer and fewer defects. Such over-testing only leads to higher IT costs and diminishing returns.

When used in conjunction with SAP Solution Manager, the SAP Quality Center application by HP and SAP LoadRunner application by HP can help you strike the right balance. By themselves, both applications support an end-to-end approach to testing that adheres to ITIL recommendations for managing the application lifecycle to meet business needs. SAP Quality Center, for example, supports comprehensive, automated, and accurate test procedures that help reduce testing costs. Whether you're gathering requirements, scheduling and running tests, managing defects, or running reports, SAP Quality Center helps ensure your new software delivers the results you paid for (Figure 2.30).

SAP LoadRunner focuses on performance, allowing you to optimize end-to-end business processes that run on SAP and non-SAP software (Figure 2.31). Using this application, you can test efficiently for normal and peak loads in a way that speeds up development schedules, reduces costs, and helps avoid project slowdowns. This helps you to more effectively mitigate risks related to SAP implementations and upgrades, as well as changes in your production systems.

When combined with SAP Solution Manager, SAP Quality Center and SAP LoadRunner can help you manage testing as a business activity that yields the greatest value at the lowest possible cost and risk. Together, these applications support a plan-drive approach to testing that is appropriate for

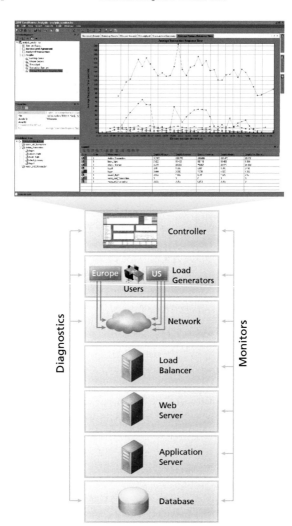

Figure 2.31 Testing application performance throughout the stack

a global quality environment or quality center of excellence environment. Plans are based on initial estimates of project scope and risk, where higher scope/risk requires more testing. Over time, you can collect testing results from various projects, store them centrally in SAP Solution Manager, and evaluate them to find process improvement insights. Based on these insights, you can fine-tune testing procedures and requirements to minimize cost and risk. This helps you to strike a balance that delivers maximum value to the business.

End-User Training and Productivity

Part of IT's job is to help end users consume its services effectively, so that the organization as a whole can deliver its business strategy. This requires a disciplined approach to end-user training that gives users what they need, when they need it. What's more, IT must be able to deliver this level of training in a way that conserves limited IT resources.

The SAP Productivity Pak application is particularly effective for addressing this challenge. This software helps your IT staff and even casual users build end-user skills using context-sensitive job aids and simulations. Content creators simply run their SAP transactions, and SAP Productivity Pak automatically records and clearly documents the process. In a single step, it creates help documents and the simulation.

Administrators can then deploy the unique output into context-sensitive online help materials that local users can access directly from their SAP software transaction screens. You can also print the materials for offline reference. This flexibility makes the application ideal for documenting your business processes and building classroom materials.

"Rapid e-learning" functionality in SAP Productivity Pak also gives your subject matter experts the ability to create effective, professional-looking tutorials without the extended learning curve associated with development

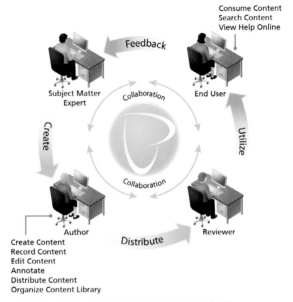

Figure 2.32 Enhanced user productivity through the content lifecycle

tools. You can even use the application to track the most-accessed training materials so that you can prioritize your training documentation requirements in future. In the end, you're able to introduce efficiencies and greater productivity into your end-to-end training processes, making both your IT staff and your user community much more productive (Figure 2.32).

End-User Monitoring

No IT organization can expect to catch all the potential problems that lead to application performance problems by monitoring technology components alone. To enable comprehensive business service availability, IT needs more. This is why so many organizations today are

supplementing their monitoring with end-user management tools such as
the SAP User Experience Management application by Knoa.

SAP User Experience Management accurately determines how each person
in your organization uses the SAP solutions your IT group has deployed.
The application provides input to comprehensive reports that you can use
to improve application response times, pinpoint training needs, adjust
business processes, and help ensure that the business is deriving the value
you expect from your SAP solutions.

In addition, SAP User Experience Management measures and reports
critical information about how people experience the actual performance
of your SAP solutions – right at their own desktops.

Using SAP User Experience Management, you'll be able to extract
actionable information about application usage, adoption, and compliance
that can help you close performance and training gaps. This, in turn, helps
to maximize training investment by linking it to actual user performance.
Ultimately, you're able to improve system performance, reduce application
errors, and minimize calls to the help desk, lowering support costs.

Correlating Business Services to IT Services

As part of SAP IT Service Management, SAP offers a service asset and
configuration management solution that supports a broad variety of use
cases. This integrated solution fulfills the requirements of a configuration
management system (CMS) that is compliant with ITIL.

Some organizations, however, may have already invested in or prefer a
configuration management database (CMDB). A CMDB, identical to
the CMS, tracks all relevant configuration items and their relationships,
for example to the higher level business services. In contrast to the fully

integrated CMS in SAP IT Service Management, the CMDB may be more appropriate for a distributed architecture (the so-called federated CMDB).

For both the integrated CMS and the CMDB, the goal is to achieve better visibility into the relationships and dependencies between business services and the IT infrastructure components that support them.

Novell CMDB360 and Novell myCMDB are CMDB solutions that can be integrated with SAP IT Service Management to provide the service desk and support staff with real-time information about the IT infrastructure. Integration is achieved through the "out of the box" SAP web service interfaces that are part of SAP IT Service Management, which can also be easily leveraged for integrating other third party CMDB products. The joint SAP and Novell solution enables you to enhance the speed and quality of incident resolution and thus leads to higher productivity and customer satisfaction.

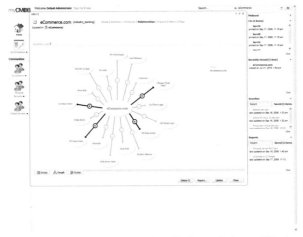

Figure 2.33 Relationship diagram showing relationships between Business and IT Services

Novell CMDB360 in particular represents the next generation in CMDB technology, providing automated capabilities that enable reconciliation, federation, visualization, and synchronization of configuration items. Automation ensures accuracy of data and configurations, compliance to standards, and auditability of change in a complex environment—all while reducing the cost of management.

Both Novell myCMDB and Novell CMDB360 complement SAP IT Service Management by enabling SAP customers to intelligently manage their SAP software infrastructure. These solutions will help your organization reduce the cost of IT management, mitigate the risk of IT change, and ensure adherence to IT governance policies throughout the enterprise. And both CMDB solutions from Novell have been SOA certified by SAP for their integration capabilities into SAP IT Service Management.

Service Diagnostics

Few events send a more negative message from IT to the business than service outages or problems that affect application performance levels. When IT fails to identify problems before they affect users, the business stands to lose in terms of revenues, decreased customer satisfaction, and damage to brand reputation.

The SAP Extended Diagnostics application by CA Wily can help. As part of the root cause analysis functionality in SAP Solution Manager, this application supports real-time application-performance monitoring so that you can detect and triage application issues proactively before SLAs are breached and users are affected. With SAP Extended Diagnostics, you can measure IT service levels, customer experience, and the associated impact on business revenue. This allows you to manage IT applications proactively and reduce customer and employee dissatisfaction while improving IT output and business benefits.

Enabling deep visibility into production environments, SAP Extended Diagnostics provides low-overhead instrumentation technology that allows you to monitor service performance even in complex service-oriented architecture (SOA) and virtualized IT landscapes. Monitoring transactions as they happen, the application identifies potential problems and evaluates the impact to the business so that IT staff can prioritize remediation activities. After an issue is detected, the application also helps determine the root cause, working as part of SAP Solution Manager to analyze the end-to-end technology stack across various standards and programming languages such as ABAP™, Java, and C++. When so much time is typically spent just in locating the source of the problem, this feature alone can significantly speed your time-to-repair rate.

Over the long term, SAP Extended Diagnostics can also be used to gather key service-level metrics and generate reports on IT performance that are

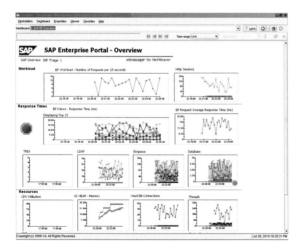

Figure 2.34 Real-time performance visibility across the stack

accessible to both technical and non-technical audiences. In the end, this enables IT to maintain system health, improve IT productivity, avoid penalties due to missed SLAs, and – most important – help the business improve satisfaction for employees and customers alike.

Streamlined Information Management

Almost everywhere, IT organizations struggle to strike the right balance when it comes to outdated legacy systems. On the one hand, the data contained in these systems is often required – whether it's for regulatory reasons, issues of proper governance, or simply for maintaining an accurate historical record. On the other hand, the cost of maintaining these legacy systems is inordinately high and the data they contain is seldom used. How do you maintain the data while minimizing your resource commitments?

The SAP Archiving application by Open Text helps to address this challenge. It helps you store data from legacy systems in a centralized location for easy access without the need to maintain the original systems. Instead of five different interfaces for five different applications, you can access all of the data through a single interface. This substantially simplifies data access throughout the organization while alleviating your staff's onerous application management duties.

The SAP Document Access application by Open Text is also available, which helps you more effectively manage unstructured information such as emails, web pages, presentations, or computer files. Your organization will be able to capture electronic and paper content in a secure archive, while maintaining easier accessibility with lower-cost storage media. This efficient approach to the management of unstructured information helps reduce administrative effort while optimizing system performance to reduce the overall total cost of ownership for your IT landscape and helping with the bottom line of the business.

Both applications integrate into your SAP software environment through
the SAP NetWeaver Information Lifecycle Management component. This
complementary component, which works with other storage applications
as well, adds a data governance engine that helps you automate data
management activities. Figure 2.35 shows how both SAP Archiving
and SAP Document Access fit into the larger, end-to-end information
management solution and process.

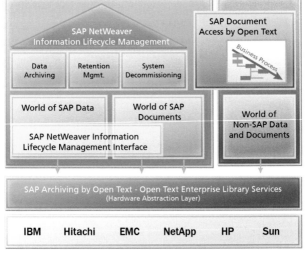

Figure 2.35 End-to-end information management solution

Summary

The idea behind solution extensions is simple: we leverage the extensive SAP ecosystem to deliver a wide range of proven solutions that integrate with your SAP software foundation to deliver fast ROI and rapid value.

The solution extensions discussed here play a critical role in helping your organization run IT as a business. From managing IT staff and generating project insights to testing software releases, monitoring service levels, and managing information more effectively, solution extensions from SAP help IT perform more effectively. Tested by SAP and pre-integrated into the SAP solution stack, these applications make it easier for you to consolidate with a single vendor so that you can focus the energies of your IT organization on accelerating business innovation and growing the business over the long term.

2.8 Solution Enablers

Sometimes, unlocking the true potential of a solution requires help. This is why SAP offers a range of solution enablers that help you get the most out of your investment. These come in the form of methodologies, training, and packaged solutions that combine software and services to minimize your risk and ensure a rapid implementation.

Rapid Deployment for SAP ITSM

You know that effective management of your IT processes is one of the key steps toward running your IT organization as a business. You may also know that the SAP ITSM application is uniquely positioned to help you manage those processes in the context of your existing SAP landscape. Yet at the same time, you may have questions about where to start with SAP ITSM, how to implement it most cost-effectively, and how to use it to realize the best results and greatest value.

Rapid deployment of SAP ITSM can help get you started at a predictable cost. With the help of experts from SAP Consulting, you can be up and running with a full ITSM solution in a matter of weeks. These experts work with you using a proven methodology that clearly outlines goals, expectations, commitments, and timelines. This helps minimize uncertainty and streamline deployment. In the end, your IT organization gets all of the robust functionality it needs to manage key ITSM processes, a growth path for future ITSM initiatives, and tailored professional services as a catalyst.

These include:
- **Consulting services** – understanding the effort, cost, risk, and scope of the final product at the very beginning of the process
- **Incident and problem management** – using functionality that supports ITIL best practices to quickly address business and technical issues as they arise within the IT context

- **Knowledge management** – consolidating knowledge from multiple sources and publishing new articles as knowledge grows
- **Web self-service** – empowering users to perform basic tasks by themselves, thereby reducing cost while enhancing the end-user experience
- **Flexible reporting** – gaining insight into the health of your IT investment with built-in flexible reporting and graphical analysis functionality
- **Growth path** – implementing optional packages for knowledge management, change management, and business intelligence, as well as SAP standard integrations for SAP Solution Manager and SAP ERP Financials

Rapid deployment of SAP ITSM is also designed to be exceptionally affordable. Only IT personnel using the full power of SAP ITSM require SAP professional user licenses. The bulk of users – the occasional requestors of IT help – do not require any licensing. This gives you the flexibility to meet your budget requirements and financial goals while still aligning core IT processes with the business to help it meet its strategic objectives.

As mentioned earlier, SAP now offers a growing number of rapid-deployment solutions that get you up and running quickly with SAP software for IT business management and many other areas.

Run SAP Methodology

SAP developed the Run SAP methodology to ensure that all customers can successfully run the systems that run their businesses. This proven methodology helps you implement and optimize solution operations, processes, and technical infrastructure across the entire solution lifecycle.

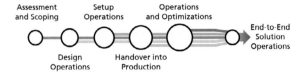

Figure 2.36: Run SAP methodology

SAP Standards for Solution Operations

The key standards and practices of the Run SAP methodology constitute
a governance framework to help you drive business value through effective
end-to-end solution operations. Content is based on global support
know-how and experience gained from thousands of installations for SAP
customers and helps you manage complexity, risk, and cost.

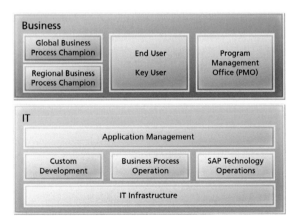

Figure 2.37 Stakeholder roles in solutions operations

The first step toward efficient end-to-end solution operations is to define clear stakeholder roles. That is why SAP has incorporated the organizational model described above into the Run SAP methodology. Comprising business and IT roles, this model:

- Serves as the foundation for efficient management of any kind of business solutions
- Facilitates collaboration among organizational units
- Highlights key considerations for processes that may be out-tasked or outsourced

Business-side roles in the organizational model are shown in Table 2.1; IT roles are shown in Table 2.2.

Business process champions	Have the lead role within the business units and define how business processes are executed
End-users	Are stakeholders who rely on implemented functionality to run their daily business
Key users	Have special knowledge of business applications and provide first-level support for colleagues
Program management office	Communicates requirements to the IT organization, decides financing for development and operations, and helps ensure implementation of requirements

Table 2.1 Business-side roles in the organizational model

Application management	Implements business requirements and supports end users
Custom development	Adjusts the solution to meet customer-specific requirements with special internal developments
Business process operations	Monitors and supports business applications, their integration, and job automation
SAP technical operations	Provides system administration and detailed system diagnostics
IT infrastructure	Provides the underlying technology including databases and networks

Table 2.2 IT roles in the organizational model

This predefined model helps you organize the core expertise essential to effective end-to-end solution operations.

End-to-end solution operations will play a critical role in delivering business value with your SAP solutions. As mentioned earlier, effective operations rely on the right organization and proven procedures. Implementing end-to-end solution operations is a vital and complex project that features a range of stakeholders – the company, system integrators, the support organization, outsourcing partners, and hardware partners. Tight coordination of the activities and resources within this project is essential to successful implementation of the solution operations you'll rely on every day.

Figure 2.38 Road map for Run SAP methodology

To aid you in this task, SAP provides a road map for Run SAP methodology to guide you through implementation (Figure 2.38). Complementary to the organizational model and standards for solution operations, this road map leads you through defining the scope of the operations to be implemented, preparing a detailed plan, doing the setup, and running your SAP and related business solutions. Moreover, it helps you find the right strategy and tools to implement your end-to-end solution operations.

Based on experience with thousands of implementations, the road map offers guidance on what needs to be implemented and how, provided in the following form:

- **Implementation methodology documents** that describe how support is implemented across the lifecycle
- **Best-practices documents** that detail how to implement the end-to-end operation of different SAP solutions based on the experiences of thousands of companies.

SAP Best Practices

For the past three decades, SAP has collaborated with successful customers and partners to develop best-practice business processes. SAP Best Practices packages offer a sound foundation for preconfigured, ready-to-use business solutions and help exploit the full potential of the SAP Business Suite. These free packages support tried-and-true business processes and are available in industry-specific as well as cross-industry versions. They can help you control costs, reduce risk, and drive more value from your SAP solutions.

SAP Best Practices packages feature:
- **A proven methodology** that leverages a reusable prototype approach to implementation
- **Support for thoroughly documented scenarios** that detail both business and technical perspectives
- **Proven preconfigurations** for SAP solutions
- **Guidelines for adapting SAP techniques** to meet your organization's specific requirements and to develop customized SAP and non-SAP hosted solutions

Training and Education

Though sometimes overlooked in the rush to go live, training is a critical component of any IT implementation. And because proper training and education can mean the difference between end-user adoption and end-user resistance, organizations who approach it as an afterthought put the success of their implementations at risk.

Unfortunately, the general market perception of standard-fare training offerings has a lot to do with the fact that organizations often put this key activity off until the last minute. In the past, training meant shipping entire teams off to remote locations while business came to a standstill. This meant expensive travel costs and lost opportunities for the business. In today's economy, companies need more options.

With training and education delivered by the SAP Education organization, you can tailor your training to meet your needs and your budget. Maintaining a comprehensive and continually evolving catalog of learning offerings, SAP Education delivers a wide range of options based on solution, role, or program.

SAP Business Suite training	**Platform training**
SAP Customer Relationship Management application	SAP NetWeaver technology platform
SAP ERP application	SAP Solution Manager application management solution
SAP Product Lifecycle Management application	Service-oriented architecture
SAP Supply Chain Management application	**Additional topics**
SAP Supplier Relationship Management application	SAP BusinessObjects solutions for enterprise performance management
SAP BusinessObjects portfolio training	SAP BusinessObjects solutions for governance, risk, and compliance
Administration	Industry-specific training
Business intelligence	
Data services	
Financial performance management	

Table 2.3 A small sample of SAP Education offering

Training can be conducted live at your site, from an SAP or partner training center, online, or through a blended-learning model that combines all of these to meet your training needs. In addition, SAP Education products and services help you share knowledge across your organization so that you can get the most value from your investment.

SAP Education also offers certifications and customized, industry-based education solutions. Plus, you'll find market-leading education choices for corporate learning, talent management, and web-based communication.

By offering training in a variety of media, formats, and access models, SAP Education helps you lower the total cost of ownership and increase the return on investment of your SAP software. You'll be able to:

- Optimize the value of your IT investment
- Reduce total cost of ownership
- Facilitate adoption and system use among your critical end users
- Manage your enterprise-wide knowledge transfer and communication

2.9   SAP Ecosystem

Every day, IT organizations are tasked to deliver results rapidly, capably, and cost-effectively with shifting business requirements and competing investment priorities. This degree of agility must be driven by fresh ideas and innovation, which comes most effectively through strong collaboration with solution providers, peers, and partners.

The SAP ecosystem responds to this growing need for a more collaborative business approach that places the customer at the center. SAP orchestrates a vast, worldwide network that includes SAP, peers, partners, and individuals – all of whom customers can turn to for the latest ideas, services, and solutions to help improve performance, decrease time to market, and enhance the business value of IT capability.

Key components in the SAP ecosystem are:
- **Partners** – certified providers to extend the value of SAP solutions and services
- **The SAP EcoHub site** – a robust, centralized information repository of SAP and partner solutions
- **Communities of innovation** – forums to facilitate and exploit the collective power of experts, partners, customers, and developers
- **The SAP Co-Innovation Lab** – a dynamic global network of partners, customers, and SAP experts incubating new ideas

The SAP ecosystem comprises a diverse collection of business and IT professionals facing similar challenges in managing the business of IT. Within the ecosystem, they connect to collaborate and co-innovate in fluid forums where timely information is always dynamic, agile, and accessible. The ecosystem's customer, partner, and developer communities are among the most vibrant and active in the industry, connecting millions of users around the world each day to foster sharing of knowledge, feedback, and solutions.

The SAP ecosystem helps you manage the business of IT by:

- Facilitating easy access to new ideas, insight, and expertise from SAP experts, peers, and partners
- Making it easier for you to identify proven partners and solutions to enhance existing capabilities
- Providing a vehicle for co-innovating new solutions to address specific business needs

Partners

SAP recognizes the vital role our partners play in helping SAP customers deliver business value through IT and has therefore created a unique partner environment. Our partner programs provide a strong foundation of support and collaboration that fosters excellent value and mutual business success for customers, partners, and SAP.

SAP partners operate in a unique environment that encourages sharing and collaboration. Partner solutions become part of the "whole" solution for customers, a model that provides customers with innovative solutions at lower costs.

SAP partners share our commitment to customer success and cover a wide range of specialties to help customers achieve that success:

- **Hosting partners** offer hosting services for SAP Business Suite applications and the SAP NetWeaver technology platform, including application management services
- **Service partners** help SAP customers design, implement, and integrate SAP solutions; optimize business and IT processes; and provide strategic business consultation
- **Software solution partners** offer SAP-certified solution extensions that integrate with and extend the value of SAP solutions (see the section "Solution Extensions")

- **Technology partners** provide infrastructure for SAP solutions, including hardware platforms, databases, storage systems, networks, and mobile devices
- **Certified providers of business process outsourcing services** deliver outsourced business functions based on SAP solutions

Additionally, official partnership programs exist in the areas of content (intellectual property or information services), education (professional training), support, and distribution channels to better serve small and midsize companies.

SAP EcoHub

SAP EcoHub centralizes information about SAP and partner solutions, enabling you to gain important knowledge and insight to support software investment decisions. The site's 360-degree view of offerings features feedback, ratings, and demonstrations to help you discover, evaluate, and buy solutions to complement your SAP investment. You can also review certification levels of SAP partner solutions and better understand integration requirements before you buy. Figure 2.39 shows the SAP EcoHub landing page for application lifecycle management and the ten best-practice IT processes discussed in the ALM section of this book.

The convergence in SAP EcoHub of rich, easy-to-access solution information and community context provides important business benefits to IT decision makers, including:

- More rapid identification of the right SAP and partner solutions for your specific business demands
- Better investment decisions, through taking advantage of expert opinions and SAP community rankings
- Less integration risk, by locating proven partners and certified solutions
- Efficient and expedited procurement, thanks to a reliable, unbiased information source

Figure 2.39 Application Lifecycle Management on SAP EcoHub

Communities of Innovation

Communities of innovation distinguish SAP as the leader in coordinating and harnessing the collective power of business experts, partners, customers, developers, and others integral to the shared success of each community. Collectively, these communities work collaboratively to help you connect quickly with expertise and resources to accelerate innovation and maximize the business value of IT.

With more than 1.6 million registered users, more than 6,000 daily forum posts, and an average question-response time of less than 20 minutes, the SAP Developer Network (SDN) site is SAP's largest community of innovation. SAP IT professionals of all kinds use SDN to connect, contribute, and co-innovate with peers using a combination of vigorous discussion forums, blogs, and Wikis. SDN members can access expert advice, follow up on business opportunities, and learn about leading-edge technologies with the potential to create greater business value through IT.

One community of innovation is covered here because of its particular relevance to the business of IT: the application lifecycle management community.

ALM Community of Innovation

SAP understands the business value of ALM and how it can drive faster development and better operation of innovative, high-quality business solutions and with lower total cost of ownership. Therefore, SAP has launched an ALM community of innovation to help customers derive full value from ALM as the go-to information and collaboration portal on this topic.

The ALM community features a robust knowledge center that provides access to:
- Practical guidance on ALM strategy, business benefits, and implementation planning
- A portfolio of best practice processes and methodologies to support ALM projects and solution operations throughout the entire lifecycle
- Detailed guidance on technical enablement of ALM
- A library of articles, white papers, and documentation
- Links to SAP and third-party tools as well as relevant SAP services
- Active, moderated forums and blogs that provide expert answers to your questions quickly

Figure 2.40 ALM community of innovation

Green IT and the SAP Co-Innovation Lab

Green IT – the practice of managing the IT asset lifecycle in a way that minimizes energy and resource consumption as well as waste – is an idea that is entering the consciousness of business and IT organizations everywhere. This is true for two reasons. First, green IT initiatives contribute directly to a company's sustainability efforts and the related impact on business results and business KPIs. For now, such initiatives are voluntary, but as issues of energy consumption and waste become more and more important, government regulation may make them mandatory, tying IT even closer to business outcome.

Second, green IT initiatives can contribute directly to significant IT cost reductions and lower business risk. By consolidating data centers, for example, organizations can significantly reduce energy consumption and carbon emissions. This can cut cooling costs dramatically. Furthermore, IT organizations that dispose of IT assets in an approved manner according to green IT policies can minimize the potential hazards of adding harmful materials such as lead and mercury to landfills. A lax approach to the disposal of such assets, on the other hand, could expose the business to the risk of fines, legal action, and negative media attention.

Given the importance of green IT, SAP has taken significant strides to help customers meet their objectives. The SAP approach to green IT is based on the following three pillars:

- **Energy** – focusing on reducing energy consumption through IT asset consolidation using techniques such as virtualization and decommissioning of legacy systems
- **E-waste** – focusing on minimizing waste through sustainable sourcing, recycling, and preventing contamination through careful salvaging techniques that properly dispose of harmful materials in a controlled manner
- **Dematerialization** – focusing on substituting high-carbon products and activities with low-carbon alternatives such as video conferencing, telecommuting, and electronic paper processes

While SAP is not a hardware vendor, we add value to green IT initiatives by supporting processes for tracking IT asset usage, managing waste, executing the logistics involved in disposal, and calculating the carbon footprint of your supply chain. In addition, SAP has worked assiduously with hardware vendors and other partners through the green IT community to help our customers become as green as possible. For example, SAP has developed a new benchmark for calculating standard hardware power consumption in relation to the size of a SAP software installation. This makes it easier for SAP, hardware vendors, and customers alike to quickly estimate power consumption probabilities as a starting point for how to best configure their SAP environments to meet green IT objectives.

SAP is also working with some of its partners through the SAP Co-Innovation Lab to develop specific green IT solutions. This lab is a hands-on environment where SAP experts, independent software vendors, system integrators, and technology providers work together with customers to develop innovative business solutions that can help solve problems that might otherwise be too complex or expensive for partners and customers to solve on their own.

One collaborative effort through the SAP Co-Innovation Lab has already produced green IT results. Working with partners in the green IT community, SAP has developed a best practice for calculating the carbon impact of a data center.

One aspect of this best practice is to populate the SAP Carbon Impact OnDemand solution with energy-related data from the data center and SAP Solution Manager. The SAP solution then takes this raw data and translates it into a carbon-impact number, even taking the type of consumed power into consideration in the calculation. This lets businesses credibly measure and compare carbon intensity across IT operations, as well as establish reduction targets and execute the most effective abatement strategies.

Another aspect resulting from the same collaborative effort provides similar functionality in an on-premise context. This leverages more robust analytics functionality to drill down into granular consumption data of all kind across the data center. This allows companies to gain even more insight into their green IT and overarching sustainability initiatives.

These best practices bring partner expertise with energy data together with SAP's expertise in translating such information into meaningful business terms. And this helps customers gain the insight they need to measure, mitigate, and monetize greenhouse gas emissions and other environmental impacts more clearly across their internal operations and supply chains. Through the SAP Co-Innovation Lab and other collaborative efforts with the SAP ecosystem and partners, SAP continues to advance the cause of green IT while helping IT organizations themselves operate more effectively to meet the needs of the business.

3. THE ROAD FORWARD

SAP approaches the business of IT as a natural extension of its core expertise in the management of highly flexible business processes that enable companies to manage their business more effectively and more efficiently. We recognize that process-driven IT is a requirement for any IT organization that wants to add value to the business. Therefore, SAP approaches the IT management market with a level of seriousness and determination commensurate to the potential value it holds for our customers everywhere.

Managing IT as a business, however, is an emerging space, and work remains to be done for IT to truly transform itself into a meaningful business function. The SAP approach to helping IT organizations move forward on this front has been two-pronged.

On one hand, we focus considerable energy on the upper end of the technology stack shown in Figure 3.1 to provide specific solutions that help put a business lens on IT management processes and data. Here the goal is to provide a CIO cockpit that supports insight and control so that IT organizations can push the envelope of IT management and deliver greater business value on a consistent basis.

On the other hand, we collaborate with a broad array of partners in the SAP ecosystem to help ensure that our solutions integrate with theirs. This follows our belief in openness and choice in the market; it also is the best way to ensure that SAP customers can preserve the investment they have already made, while they adopt the IT Business Management offering from SAP in combination.

It is imperative, however, to approach the entire stack as an integrated entity. To this end, SAP is moving forward on various fronts. For example, one objective is to more tightly integrate SAP IT Service Management with SAP Solution Manager – which, in turn, will help organizations more effectively manage the end-to-end application lifecycle. Integration at this level, for instance, will help your IT organization to move seamlessly from root cause analysis for problems into workflow that leads to problem resolution.

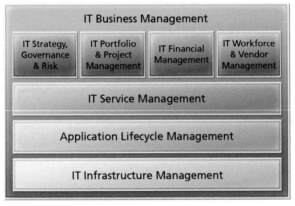

Figure 3.1 IT management stack as integrated entity

Cloud computing is another area of focus for SAP. This is a transformative shift for IT organizations everywhere, and SAP plans to make its solutions for managing the business of IT fully cloud-ready. For SAP, however, this means much more than just enabling virtualization. More important, it means enabling IT to make sound business decisions about when and why to move applications to the cloud. SAP envisions a cloud management cockpit that allows IT managers to assess cloud options in the context of cost, risk, quality of service, and the needs of the business. Based on such criteria, IT can focus less on the technology behind cloud computing and more on the value that it delivers to the business (see Figure 3.2).

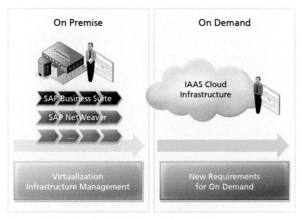

Figure 3.2 On demand – technical and business challenge for IT

In the end, SAP envisions a fully integrated set of tools that help break down IT barriers to create a single source of truth that delivers insight into IT processes and helps IT manage itself more effectively as a business. Integration, however, does not mean a single monolithic solution for all organizations at all times. In a world where one size does not fit all, SAP sees its role as providing the glue that binds critical IT processes together. SAP has built its reputation doing exactly this in the area of traditional business processes, working successfully with companies in all corners of the globe for more than three decades. Bringing this unparalleled expertise to bear on how IT manages its activities, SAP aims to help your IT organization transform itself from a provider of technology to a full-fledged business partner with a voice at the executive table, devising strategies and delivering solutions that generate measurable business value and contribute to business success.